# Tiny Boxes

DOUG STOWE

# Tiny
# Boxes

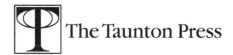

The Taunton Press

The Taunton Press
Inspiration for hands-on living®

The Taunton Press, Inc., 63 South Main Street, PO Box 5506, Newtown, CT 06470-5506
e-mail: tp@taunton.com

Editor: Christina Glennon
Copy Editor: Seth Reichgott
Cover design: Carol Singer / www.carol-singer-design.com
Interior design: Kimberly Adis
Layout: Carol Singer / www.carol-singer-design.com
Illustrator: Christopher Mills
Photographer: Doug Stowe, except for photos on cover, pp. ii, 2 (right), 3, 4, 15, 34, 50, 60,
73, 94, 109, 122 by Scott Phillips

Library of Congress Cataloging-in-Publication Data

Names: Stowe, Doug, author.
Title: Tiny boxes / Doug Stowe.
Description: Newtown, CT : The Taunton Press, Inc., [2016]
Identifiers: LCCN 2016034557 | ISBN 9781631864476
Subjects: LCSH: Woodwork. | Wooden boxes. | Box making,
Classification: LCC TT197.5.B68 .S 764 2016 | DDC 745.593--dc23
LC record available at https://lccn.loc.gov/2016034557

Printed in the United States of America
10 9 8 7 6 5 4 3 2 1

The following manufacturers/names appearing in *Tiny Boxes* are trademarks:
Amana Tool®, Lee Valley®, Masonite®, Nexabond™

About Your Safety: Working wood is inherently dangerous. Using hand or power tools improperly or ignoring safety practices can lead to permanent injury or even death. Don't try to perform operations you learn about here (or elsewhere) unless you're certain they are safe for you. If something about an operation doesn't feel right, don't do it. Look for another way. We want you to enjoy the craft, so please keep safety foremost in your mind whenever you're in the shop.

*To my wife Jean*

## ACKNOWLEDGMENTS

**A GOOD BOOK IS ALWAYS A TEAM EFFORT.**
I offer my sincere thanks to these folks at The Taunton Press:

Peter Chapman, acquisitions editor
Christina Glennon, editor
Rosalind Loeb Wanke, art director
Carol Singer, cover design
Scott Phillips, photographer
And the illustrator, Christopher Mills

# Contents

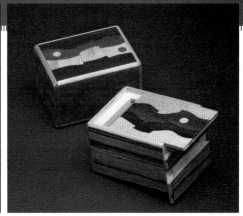

# INTRODUCTION

**TINY BOXES REQUIRE LITTLE IN THE WAY** of material, and their small size makes unnecessary some of the complex joinery techniques used on larger boxes. But as you can probably tell from the photos in this book, tiny boxes can present a craftsman's challenge equal to that offered by their larger counterparts. They can also be as beautiful and as interesting. You can make them using a wide range of techniques, yet you need not have a fully equipped shop.

Tiny boxes can be quickly and easily made, provided you know the means to safely handle and craft the very small parts involved. Throughout this book I have tried to illustrate techniques that will not only save you time but also ensure you can build these boxes safely. Because of their size and the techniques used to make them, the boxes invite you to make several at once, thus ensuring that you'll have small gifts for nearly any occasion and still have some left to keep and treasure yourself.

Tiny boxes like these have been some of my favorites to make, and I truly hope that you, too, will find pleasure and success in making these designs.

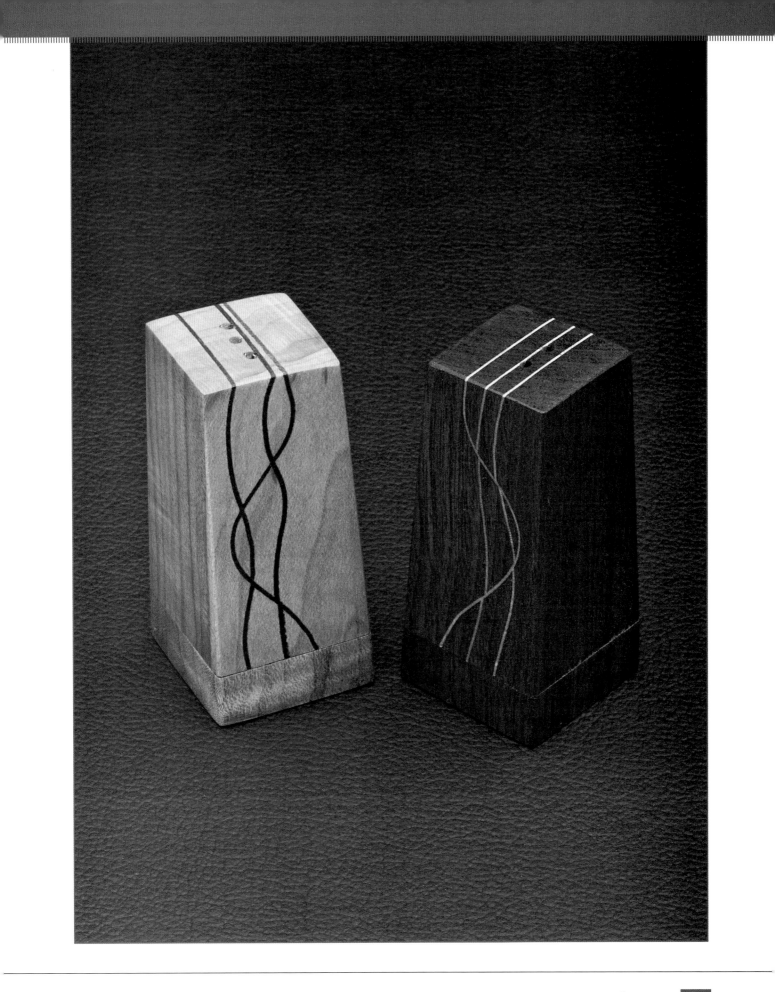

# A Bandsawn Box

**B**ANDSAWN BOXES are extremely easy and fun to make. All you need are a bandsaw (or scrollsaw for the smallest sizes), a ⅛-in. blade to turn through tight curves, a chunk of wood, and some imagination. Chunks of wood can be glued up from thinner stock, but I prefer to work with thicker materials because they provide me with more design options. Burled woods like the myrtle used in the primary project in this chapter display incredible beauty. But as you will see in the variations at the end of the chapter, even a chunk of oak firewood can make an interesting box. In fact, a single piece of firewood can make several boxes, each one unique. You will also be surprised by how quickly a bandsawn box can go from idea to finished form.

Begin by carefully selecting your stock. The myrtle used to make this box came from a leftover slab from a veneer mill in South Carolina, and was one that I bought years ago because it was cheap, beautiful, and I knew it would someday be useful in making a box. This particular piece of wood had a badly weathered edge that made it of little value for veneer making, but of great value for boxmaking. I like the various textures of wood, and the imperfections offer design opportunities, making for an interesting final piece.

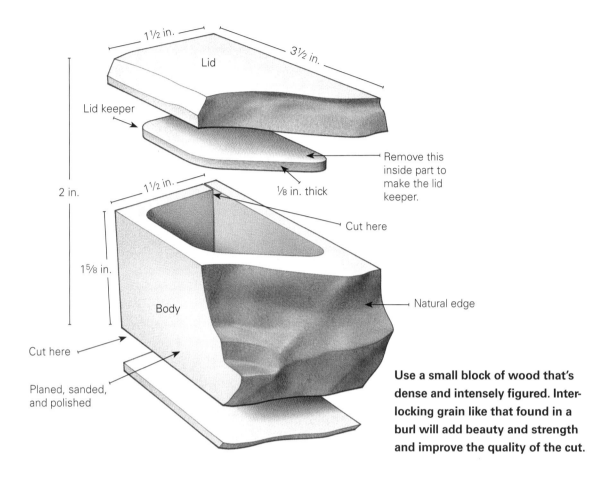

1½ in.

Lid

3½ in.

Lid keeper

Remove this inside part to make the lid keeper.

⅛ in. thick

2 in.

1½ in.

Cut here

1⅝ in.

Natural edge

Body

Cut here

Planed, sanded, and polished

**Use a small block of wood that's dense and intensely figured. Interlocking grain like that found in a burl will add beauty and strength and improve the quality of the cut.**

# Prepare the stock

**IN ORDER TO TURN A CHUNK OF WOOD INTO** a finished box, first the bottom and lid must be cut away from the body of the box to create the various box components.

**1.** To remove the bottom, set the fence on the bandsaw to cut a slice about ⅛ in. thick. You can use a fence on the bandsaw to get a straight cut, as I do here **(PHOTO A, PHOTO B on p. 6)** but simply marking a line and making a freehand cut will suffice.

A

**USE THE BANDSAW to make your first cut. Remove a thin slice from the base of the stock to create the bottom.**

**THE THICKNESS OF THE CUT** is your choice, but it can be ⅛ in. or even less on a tiny bandsawn box.

**2.** Move the fence on the bandsaw far enough away from the blade to cut the lid from the body of the box. How far you set it will depend on how large your initial block of wood is and how thick you want your lid to be **(PHOTO C)**. The photo below **(PHOTO D)** shows the layers as they were removed from the initial chunk.

**MAKE YOUR SECOND CUT** to remove the lid from the body of the box. You can either use the fence for a straight cut or simply freehand the cut for a more irregular effect.

**YOUR FIRST CUTS REVEAL** the hidden potential of the wood, as shown in this myrtle burl.

# Hollow the inside

**THE INSIDE OF THE REMAINING CHUNK OF** wood must be cut away to form the interior space of the box. Next, for the lid to fit into an exact spot, a "lid keeper" must be cut from the waste that came from the inside of the box.

**1.** Sketch a line to help you plan the cut you will make to hollow out the inside of the box. Avoid overly tight turns that would bind the blade as it travels through the wood. With a ⅛-in. blade on the bandsaw, a radius of ⅜ in. is manageable, but tighter curves will put a strain on the blade and shorten its life. (A scrollsaw can make much tighter cuts, as you will see on p. 14.)

**2.** Make a cut from outside the box straight in, and then follow the shape you have outlined. When you've cut all the way back to the starting line, turn the saw off and carefully back the blade out of the cut **(PHOTOS A & B )**.

**3.** After the inside is cut from the body of the box, all that remains is to cut a keeper piece for the lid and to assemble the box. From the piece left over from inside the body of the box, cut a thin slice from the top side to form the lid keeper. To safely cut such a small part, use a push block to guide the material through the cut. I make the lid keeper piece about ⅛ in. thick **(PHOTO C )**.

**MAKE A STRAIGHT CUT** into the end of the box with the bandsaw and then follow your pencil line to remove the interior material to form the inside of the box.

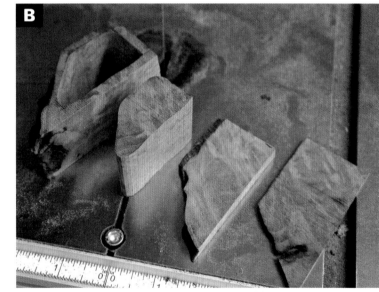

**SHOWN LEFT TO RIGHT,** the body of the box, the material cut away from the interior, the lid, and the bottom of the box.

**USE THE BANDSAW** to cut a thin slice from the top of the piece removed from the body of the box. This thin slice is the lid keeper.

# Assemble the box

1. To prepare for assembly, first place the body of the box upside down on the lid and align both pieces, then trace the shape of the body of the box on the lid so that you will know where to glue the keeper to the lid (**PHOTO A**).

2. Spread glue on the lid keeper and press it in place on the underside of the lid, positioned within the pencil line you just traced from the body of the box (**PHOTO B**). Use clamps to hold the keeper in place as the glue sets.

3. To begin assembly of the body of the box, first use a business card or candy wrapper to spread glue into the cut that you made at the end of the box (**PHOTO C**). Use a clamp to close that small cut.

**PLACE THE BODY OF THE BOX** upside down on the lid and use a pencil to trace the inside shape.

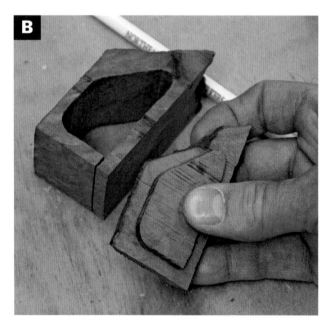

**APPLY GLUE TO THE UNDERSIDE** of the lid keeper and glue it carefully to the lid within the traced outline of the interior of the box. Use clamps to hold it in place as the glue dries.

**USE A BUSINESS CARD** or candy wrapper to spread glue into the bandsaw kerf where you first cut in to form the inside of the box. I put a bit of glue on the card and simply pull it out so the glue spreads.

**4.** Once the glue in the small cut has dried, apply glue to the underside of the body of the box in order to glue the bottom in place **(PHOTO D )**.

**5.** Use small clamps to hold the bottom in place while the glue sets **(PHOTO E )**. Check carefully that the edges are aligned before you set the assembly aside to dry.

**APPLY GLUE** to the bottom edge of the body of the box in order to glue the bottom in place (above).

**USE CLAMPS** to hold the bottom in place as the glue dries (left).

# Sanding and finishing

**YOU MAY CHOOSE TO USE A STATIONARY** belt sander to sand your bandsawn box, as shown at right. Similar results can be achieved on such a small box with a piece of self-adhesive sandpaper affixed to the workbench or to a sanding block.

**ONE SANDING OPTION** is to use a stationary belt sander to smooth the flat edges.

The sanding and finishing techniques you use on your bandsawn box will depend on the materials and the chosen shape. A flat sheet of sandpaper mounted to a flat surface or wrapped around a sanding block can be quite effective on a small box. Use a spindle sander (**PHOTO A**) or a large dowel wrapped in fine-grit sandpaper to smooth inside curved cuts (**PHOTO B**). Flat surfaces can also be approached with a random-orbit power sander for quick results. Move through grits from coarse to fine (**PHOTO C**).

I am careful not to remove too much in my sanding operations. Leaving some textures from the natural wood can make the finished box more appealing than if they were simply sanded away. For instance, in the photo at bottom right (**PHOTO D**), the boxes at left and right have textures that were present in the wood, whereas in the smaller box at center I've kept the bandsawn marks that were left when this box was cut from the inside of the box to its left.

**USE A SPINDLE SANDER** to smooth inside curved cuts.

**A DOWEL WRAPPED** with fine sandpaper can polish curved surfaces.

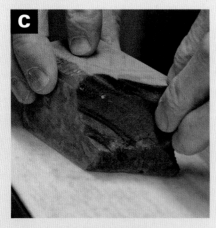

**USE A RANDOM-ORBIT SANDER** to sand the box through the finer grits. I use 180-grit, 240-grit, and finish with 320-grit sandpaper before applying the finish.

**DON'T SAND AWAY ALL** the interesting textures. The various textures on these boxes, whether of natural origin or left by tools, can add spice to the finished boxes.

# Spalted Maple Box with a Leather Lining

**Interesting linings can be cut at the same time you make a box,
as shown in this spalted maple example.**

**1.** Apply a layer of double-faced tape to the bottom of what will become the inside of the box **(PHOTO A )**.

**2.** Stick a piece of leather to the double-faced tape and carefully spread the leather over the tape **(PHOTO B )**.

**3.** On the bandsaw, cut to remove the inside of the box, as you did with the main box. The lining for the bottom of the box will be cut to fit at the same time **(PHOTO C )**.

**4.** The leather will require a bit of trimming on the edges with scissors to remove the fuzz, but the lining will be a perfect fit **(PHOTO D )**. Use wood glue to attach the leather to the inside bottom of the box after assembly.

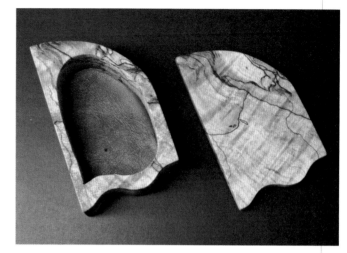

**THE FINAL SPALTED MAPLE BOX** with the lining in place.

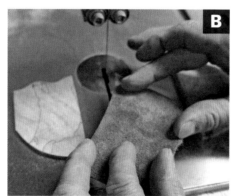

**USE DOUBLE-FACED TAPE** to affix a leather lining to what will become the inside of the box (far left).

**SPREAD THE LEATHER CAREFULLY** to make sure it sticks (left).

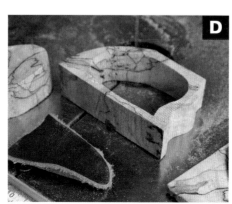

**USE THE BANDSAW** to cut the shape of the interior of the box, cutting the leather lining at the same time (far left).

**THE LEATHER WILL REQUIRE** just a bit of trimming with scissors to remove the fuzzy edge, but this box made from spalted maple is ready for assembly (left).

# A Surprising Rustic Firewood Box

**Wood for bandsawn boxes can come from the most unlikely places. As an example, this box came from my stack of firewood, split and ready for next winter's warmth.**

**CUT THE FIREWOOD** to the height of your box.

**1.** Cut one end off the stick of firewood, at about the height of your intended box **(PHOTO A )**.

**2.** Remove a thin slice from one end to form the bottom of the box **(PHOTO B )**.

**3.** Remove the lid in the same manner, but leave it thicker. Note that whereas the bottom was a straight cut, I put a curve in the underside of the lid to add interest.

**4.** Use the bandsaw to remove stock from the interior **(PHOTO C )**. Cut straight in on one end, then follow gentle curves around the remaining three corners.

**5.** Cut a lid keeper from the waste and then this box will be ready for assembly **(PHOTO D )**.

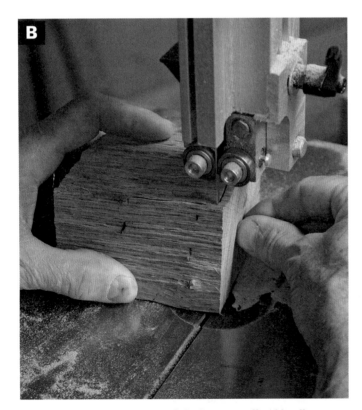

**TO FORM THE BOTTOM** of the box, cut off a thin slice.

**WITH THE BANDSAW,** cut to form the interior of the box.

**6.** Use glue and clamps to assemble the box pieces. Make certain the edges are carefully aligned **(PHOTO E )**.

**7.** Rather than sand this box, I used a wire brush to remove some of the fibers that were left loose when I split the log into firewood **(PHOTO F )**.

**8.** Gently round the crisp edges with sandpaper. A lovely rustic box is the result.

**USE A WIRE BRUSH** to remove loose
fibers from the outside of the box.

**RUSTIC ELEGANCE**
in a useful box

## VARIATIONS ON A SIMPLE THEME

**THE BANDSAW technique used in this chapter can be used to make a variety of boxes. Changing the wood used, the shapes cut, and the finishing dramatically changes the finished product.**

Each piece of wood you choose for making a bandsawn box can bring interesting results. Made from a small block of olive burl, the box at right is made using the same techniques as the main box (the piece in the background in the photo became an even smaller box on its own through the use of the scrollsaw).

**EXPERIMENT WITH OTHER SHAPES, woods, and sizes, and take your lead from what you find in the patterns in the wood. This box is cut from olive burl.**

**SOMETIMES WHAT IS CUT from the inside of a box can become an even smaller box. This one was created using a scrollsaw. The parts were cut from what remained from the box shown above.**

# A Hinged Pocket Box

A tiny hinged pocket box is the perfect place to carry small treasures or something more appropriately kept at hand, like pills needed for a day away from home. It's also the perfect place to stash a pair of earrings to keep them from becoming tangled in your purse. For woodworkers, this box is a perfect way to develop precision and use small bits of beautiful wood that would otherwise go in the landfill. With this box, the precise opening on copper pins and the way the lid snaps securely shut on tiny rare earth magnets make it a delight to hold, to open, and to use.

This small box defies some rules of boxmaking. Elaborate corner joining techniques are often used to construct a box. But the very small amount of contraction and expansion caused by changes in humidity makes anything more than just glue overkill in making this box's secure joints. In fact, I have had small boxes made using this glue-only technique last for 40 years without coming apart.

Success in making this box will not come without some effort in building what you need to do the job right. But it's worth it, because this tiny box will launch you into making your own inlay, giving you the capability to enhance all of your future projects with an extra level of craftsmanship.

# Hinged Pocket Box

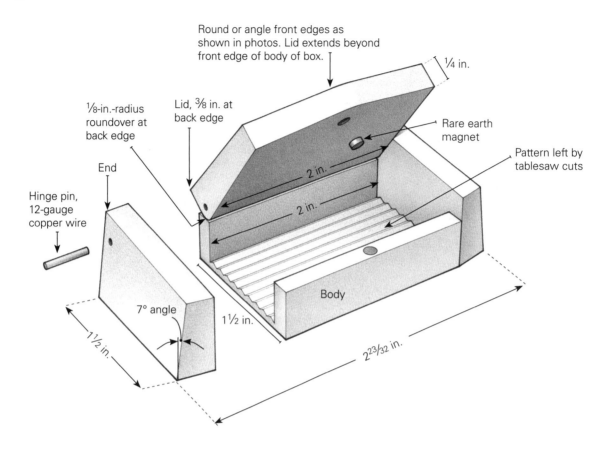

Round or angle front edges as shown in photos. Lid extends beyond front edge of body of box.

¼ in.

⅛-in.-radius roundover at back edge

Lid, ⅜ in. at back edge

Rare earth magnet

Pattern left by tablesaw cuts

End

2 in.

2 in.

Hinge pin, 12-gauge copper wire

Body

7° angle

1½ in.

1½ in.

2²³⁄₃₂ in.

## MATERIALS

| QUANTITY | PART | MATERIAL | SIZE | NOTES |
| --- | --- | --- | --- | --- |
| 1 | Body | Cherry or maple | ½ in. x 1½ in. x 2 in. | Cut several from longer stock |
| 2 | Ends | Cherry or maple | ⅜ in. x ¹⁵⁄₁₆ in.* x 1½ in. | Tapered at 7-degree angle |
| 1 | Lid | Cherry or maple | ⅜ in. x 1½ in. x 2 in. | Tapered toward front at 7-degree angle |
| 10 –12 Pieces | Inlay | Mixed hardwoods | ⅛ in. x 1¾ in. x 18 in. | |
| 2 | Hinge pins | 12-gauge copper wire | ¾ in. long | Strip off plastic coating |
| 2 | Rare earth magnets | | ¹⁄₁₆ in. thick x ⅛ in. diameter | www.kjmagnetics.com Number D-21 |

*Sand flush with lid after assembly.

# Start with simple inlay

**1.** Rip thin pieces of wood from various species. I used walnut, mahogany, maple, sassafras, and padauk, ripped into strips ⅛ in. thick and 1¾ in. wide. Use a push block on the tablesaw to keep your hands a safe distance from the blade **(PHOTO A )**. A zero-clearance insert in the tablesaw helps to support the stock through the cut.

**2.** When enough strips have been ripped (about 10 or 12), stack and arrange them in a pleasing pattern of alternating colors and species of wood.

To prevent wasting stock, I laid them out in a diagonal pattern (at about a 50-degree angle) and made a mark across the wood in pencil so that they could be glued and rearranged back in the same position **(PHOTO B )**.

**3.** Spread glue between the layers of wood and gradually build a block of color from the various species. Use the mark made in step 2 to align the pieces **(PHOTO C )**.

**USE THE TABLESAW** to cut thin strips for the inlay. Keep the blade set just high enough to cut through and use a push stick to control the stock safely through the cut.

**STACK THE STRIPS** in an alternating arrangement of colors. To eliminate waste, position them how you want to glue them, and then mark them so they can easily be reassembled as they are being glued.

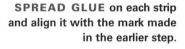

**SPREAD GLUE** on each strip and align it with the mark made in the earlier step.

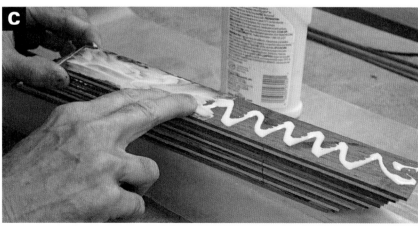

**4.** Use clamps to pull the stack of wood together tightly as the glue dries. Blocks (or cauls) wrapped in wax paper help to ensure uniform clamping pressure, and the wax paper keeps excess glue from the bench top and clamps **(PHOTO D)**.

**5.** After the glue has dried, flatten one side of the stack of veneer on the jointer **(PHOTO E)**.

**6.** Run the flattened stack through the planer so that it is surfaced evenly on both sides **(PHOTO F)**.

**7.** Using the compound miter saw to cut the pieces for the inlay has some very specific requirements for safety and accuracy, so refer to the sidebar on the facing page for safety tips. Tilt the angle of the compound miter saw to 50 degrees. Use a stop block also cut to a 50-degree angle on one end to control the length of the cut as you cut pieces from the block **(PHOTO G)**. Let the blade stop while in the full down position after each cut to prevent the

**USE STRAIGHT BLOCKS (or cauls)** on the outside of the stock as you apply pressure with clamps.

**USE THE JOINTER to flatten one side of the stock to prepare it to be cut into sections to make inlay.**

**THIS GLUED AND FLATTENED STACK** of veneers is the foundation for interesting inlay.

G

**USE A COMPOUND MITER SAW** to cut the inlay into short pieces at a 50-degree angle. The accessory fence, stop block, and correct procedure are absolutely necessary for the safety of this operation.

## SAFELY USING COMPOUND MITER SAWS FOR BOXMAKING

Compound miter saws were originally intended for rougher work by contractors and trim carpenters, therefore there are special concerns when cutting very small parts. Some of these concerns have to do with modifications made to the saw to allow for safer cuts, and others have to do with how you use the saw.

The first thing you will notice about a compound miter saw in its native condition is the amount of open space surrounding the blade at the back and in the table. The table has a gaping hole where very small parts can fall through. The center of the saw fence is relatively open, allowing for the saw to be tilted in various ways to adapt to the needs of a carpenter cutting moldings at various angles and degrees. For boxmaking, a backer board is required to provide adequate backing when making small cuts.

On my saw, I added pieces of ½-in. Baltic birch plywood on both sides of the blade, and added blue masking tape to the throat plate so that small pieces of wood would not fall through after being cut. The Baltic birch backing board also provides a secure place to clamp stop blocks to ensure an accurate cut. These are easy adjustments to make to your saw for more effective use on small boxes.

For safer and more precise cuts you'll also need to modify the way you use your saw. In the photo above material is being cut that is trapped between the blade and the stop block. In this case, the stop block is required to cut the stock to the precise 50-degree angle and length. Without the stop block in place the material would slide and be miscut. But if I were to lift the saw up after the cut with the blade still running, the material would be lifted, too, spun into the blade, forced against the stop block, chewed up, and thrown at the operator. In addition, the force of the blade would jam the stock against the stop block and make virtually certain that it would no longer be in the right spot for an accurate cut. The solution is quite simple. Stop the saw by releasing the trigger while the saw is in the down position and wait until the blade stops before lifting it from the cut. This is a hard lesson for many woodworkers to learn, but safe practice demands it of the boxmaker. This is a particularly hard lesson for those who are already familiar with the use of this tool in a more hurried environment. And while hurried use of the tool can be a challenge to unlearn, all subsequent work with this tool, even beyond boxmaking, will benefit from adhering to this simple rule.

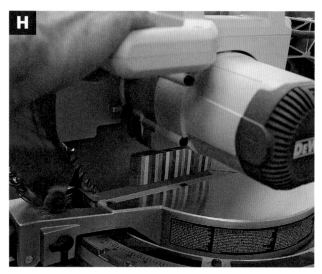

RELEASE THE TRIGGER on the saw and wait until the blade stops completely before lifting the blade. This is crucial for a safe cut.

IF GREAT CARE IS TAKEN, the results will show with accurate pieces.

SPREAD GLUE FIRST on the outer strips and then on the patterned parts as you assemble your patterned inlay strips.

cut-off stock from being lifted and chewed by the blade (PHOTO **H**). If you have been very careful in your cut, the inlay stock will remain safely on the table after the saw has stopped and been raised from the table. Masking tape was used to keep the cut-off stock from falling through the throat plate of the saw (PHOTO **I**). Cut six slices from your inlay block to make a set of inlay strips to use in your boxmaking.

**8.** Build your inlay strip on a ⅛-in. strip of wood chosen to match or contrast with the material you plan to use as the lid of your box. Because I am inlaying in a cherry lid, I chose cherry strips ⅛ in. thick and 1¾ in. wide to form the outer layers of my inlay. Spread glue on each layer as you build your inlay strip (PHOTO **J**).

**9.** Use clamps and cauls to hold the parts in alignment as the glue sets (PHOTO **K**).

**10.** After the glue has set, use the tablesaw to cut thin strips, about ³⁄₃₂ in. thick, from the block of inlay pattern. Make certain that your blade is set no higher than is required, and that you have a push stick to keep your hands safe from the blade (PHOTO **L**).

USE CLAMPS TO HOLD the inlay strips tight as they are glued together. Cauls make certain that there are no gaps and that the finished inlay strips will be straight.

USE THE TABLESAW TO CUT thin strips of patterned inlay from the block you have just made. A single strip will inlay several small pocket boxes.

# Form the body of the box

**THIS BOX HAS AN INTERESTING INTERIOR** that my customers have told me they like. It is simply formed by making a series of cuts on the tablesaw, each carefully measured at ⅛ in. apart. By making these carefully measured cuts, a corrugated surface is formed on the bottom of the box. The feature looks interesting but also serves a purpose, making it easier to grasp and lift small items from within the box.

**1.** In creating boxes like this I never make just one body at a time, because it is safer to handle longer parts on the tablesaw than it is to make the short cuts that would be required for a single box. Starting at the center of the body, make a cut on the tablesaw, leaving ⅛ in. of thickness at what will become the bottom of the box **(PHOTO )**. Move the fence in ⅛-in. increments on both sides until the full width of the interior of the box is formed (approximately 1⅛ in.).

**WORK SMART**

If you work with stock long enough to make more than one box, you will be able to work more safely and produce multiple boxes quickly and efficiently.

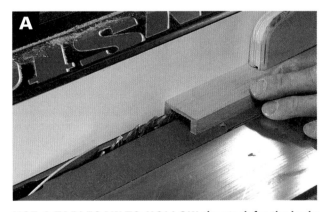

USE A TABLESAW TO HOLLOW the stock for the body of the box. The "V" cut of the blade creates an interesting corrugated effect.

**2.** Both the lid and ends can be cut from a single piece of stock. Make a cut at a 7-degree angle down the length of stock to form the lid and ends of the box. I have the blade set at a 7-degree angle so that the lids will be thicker at the back to allow for the hinge pins, and so that the ends will taper slightly up toward the top. This is done with the blade tilted and with the stock carefully guided with a push stick **(PHOTO B )**. The offcut from this operation provides the stock needed to form the ends of the box.

**3.** Cut the ends of the box to width and length and the body to length.

**4.** Use a squeeze bottle to apply glue to the ends of the body. You will notice my use of masking tape to assemble the box body and ends prior to gluing. The tape makes it much easier to hold the ends in place as glue and clamps are applied. Minor adjustments can be made only during the first few minutes and only before the glue begins to set. Leave the body of the box with the ends clamped in place to dry for an hour or more before the next steps **(PHOTO C )**.

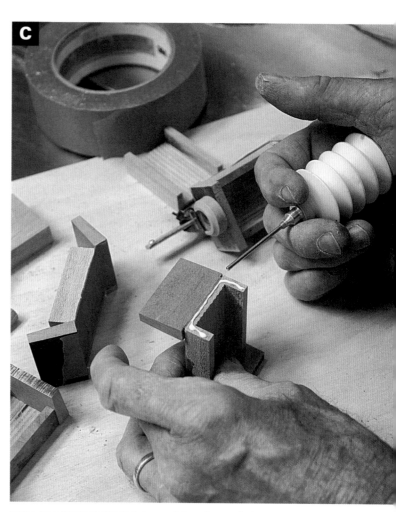

**USE THE TABLESAW** to rip stock for the lid and ends of the box.

**USE MASKING TAPE** to position the ends in place to prepare for gluing. Then apply a bead of glue to the end grain of the body of the box. Clamp the ends on tightly as the glue sets.

# Inlay the lids

**SET THE HEIGHT** of the bit in the router table so that it's not quite as high as the inlay stock is thick.

**USE A PUSH BLOCK** on the router table to rout the groove for the inlay. This will take more than one pass and requires great care to get a good fit.

**IT IS BEST TO MAKE SEVERAL OF THESE** boxes at the same time and inlay a strip of lids rather than try to deal one at a time with small parts. And of course that is one of the most important tips for successful boxmaking. Work with stock long enough to make more than one box, and you will perform your work more safely as a result.

**1.** In your router table, use a straight-cut router bit just smaller than the width of your inlay strip. Set the height of the cut at just a hair under the thickness of the inlay strip, so that when installed it will leave just a bit proud to be sanded flush **(PHOTO A )**.

**2.** Use a push block to guide the lid stock across the router table, then adjust the position of the fence to widen the cut until it fits the strip **(PHOTO B )**. If you have some variation in the width of the strip (as is quite normal), cut the width of the channel to fit the narrowest part of the strip and use a block plane to narrow the strip where necessary **(PHOTO C )**.

**WHEN INSTALLING THE INLAY** in the lid, look for a tight fit with no spaces on either side. A block plane can be used to adjust the final fit as long as the groove isn't already too wide.

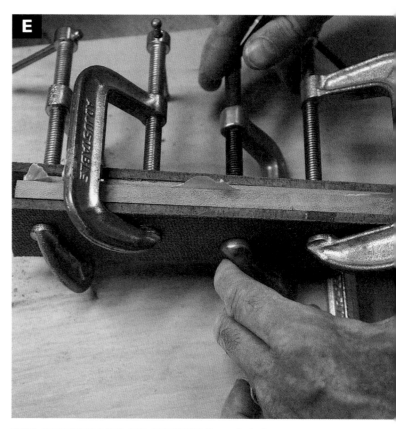

**SPREAD GLUE** in the groove and then press the inlay strips in place.

**USE HARDBOARD OR PLYWOOD** cauls to keep the clamps from marking the underside of the lids and to spread gluing pressure evenly.

**3.** Spread glue in the inlay channel and press the strip in place **(PHOTO D )**.

**4.** To clamp the inlay strip in place, align the lid stock in pairs front to front with wax paper between. The wax paper will keep the lids from sticking to each other from any glue that squeezes out. Use hardboard (Masonite®) blocking to distribute the clamping pressure and to keep the clamps from marring the lids **(PHOTO E )**.

**5.** Use either the compound miter saw or the tablesaw and sled (see the sidebar on pp. 28–29) to cut the box lids to their finished length. They should be just enough shorter than the body of the box to rotate freely within the box ends. Set a stop block, and make a test cut first (this can be on a piece of scrapwood). When you are satisfied with

the fit—the lid should fit between the ends without excessive play and without being tight—cut the lid. Use a pencil as your hold-down device to keep the lid under tight control during the cut, and to keep your hands a safe distance from the blade. As mentioned in the sidebar at on p. 19, stop the compound miter saw while it is in the full down position and wait until the blade stops before

**WORK SMART**

During glue-up, put wax paper between the caul and lids to keep them from sticking in case extra glue seeps out. An alternative technique is to apply a coat of paste wax to your caul.

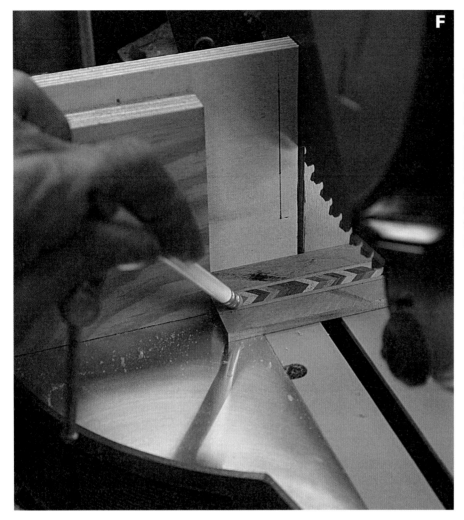

F

USE EITHER THE COMPOUND
MITER SAW or the tablesaw with
sled to cut the lid to length. With
either tool, some form of hold-
down is required to control the
piece between the stop block and
blade. The eraser end of a pencil
will offer enough control to give
a clean cut. With the compound
miter saw, allow the blade to come
to a complete stop in the down
position.

raising it and removing your lid. There is no sense
in passing the moving blade through the stock
twice, and lifting a spinning blade while the stock
is in place might damage the lid that you have
carefully inlaid **(PHOTO F )**.

**6.** The back edge of the lid must be routed with
a ⅛-in.-radius roundover bit to provide clearance
at the back so that the lid will be able to open after
the pin hinges are installed. Set the router bit
so that the height of the edge of the cut is flush
with the top of the router table and so that the
bearing is in alignment with the fence. Use a
foam-backed hold-down pad to guide the lid
through the cut **(PHOTO G )**.

G

USE A ⅛-IN. ROUNDOVER BIT
in the router table to round the back
edge of the lid.

# Install the hinge pins

**IF YOU ARE MAKING ONLY ONE OR TWO** boxes that are no more than 2 in. or 3 in. long, the holes for the hinge pins can be drilled using the drill press equipped with a fence and stop blocks. If your box is longer, you will need to make a drilling guide, as shown in the sidebar on p. 30.

**1.** Sand the ends flush with the back of the box on the disk sander. If a disk sander is not available, this job can also be accomplished on a flat piece of coarse sandpaper with a few strokes and careful attention. **(PHOTO A )**.

**2.** Setting up the drill press to drill the pin holes requires careful measuring. The hole must be ⅛ in. from the back of the box and ⅛ in. from the underside of the lid. A tape measure is an awkward means to make such important measurements, but can work if you are willing to accept some risk of failure or you could use a small square. First set the distance from the fence to the underside of the lid, as this will remain constant for the holes at both ends. Then carefully align the box in place to drill the first hole. Note that I use a business card as a shim between the body of the box and the lid. Even with the back edge of the lid routed to provide clearance for opening, the additional clearance provided by lifting the lid away from the fence an amount equal to the thickness of a business card is essential to the smooth opening and closing of the box **(PHOTO B )**.

**USE A DISK SANDER**, belt sander, or sheet of sandpaper glued to a flat board to sand the ends flush with the back of the box.

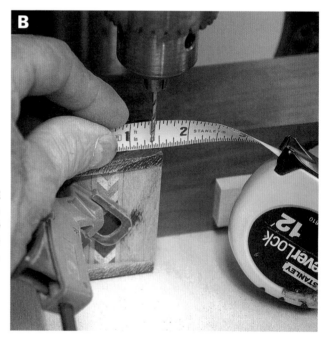

**CAREFULLY MEASURE** for the locations of the pin holes. Set up stops and the fence on the drill press to control the drilling.

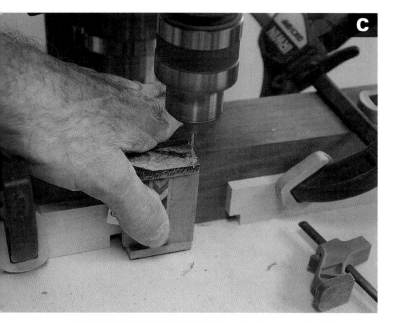

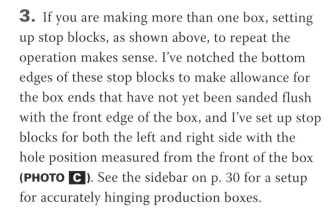

**HOLD THE BOX TIGHTLY** to the fence and to the appropriate stop for accurate drilling.

**STRIP 12-GAUGE COPPER WIRE** to use as hinge pins and use a wire cutter to snip it to the required length. I round the end of the wire slightly so it will easily enter the holes.

**3.** If you are making more than one box, setting up stop blocks, as shown above, to repeat the operation makes sense. I've notched the bottom edges of these stop blocks to make allowance for the box ends that have not yet been sanded flush with the front edge of the box, and I've set up stop blocks for both the left and right side with the hole position measured from the front of the box **(PHOTO C )**. See the sidebar on p. 30 for a setup for accurately hinging production boxes.

**4.** The hinge pins for this box are made of 12-gauge copper wire that has been stripped of its plastic cover. Those pins can be tapped in place, but left long so that they can be pulled out so the lid can be shaped and sanded and so the magnets can be installed. Clip the pins short with wire cutters when you are ready for finish sanding **(PHOTO D )**.

## CHOOSING THE RIGHT SIZE DRILL BIT

I chose two drill bits for fitting the hinge pins for this box, based on measuring the 12-gauge copper wire used for the pins. The wire measures about 0.0795 in. in diameter, so I selected a slightly smaller numbered drill (number 47) to drill the first hole to a depth of about ½ in. The diameter of that drill was 0.0785 in., so the pin would fit in tightly without splitting the wood. Then I drill a slightly larger hole with a number 46 drill bit (0.081 in. in diameter) to allow for the rotation of the pin in the box ends. This is drilled to a depth of ¼ in. less than the original hole.

One of the most important discoveries in my own box making was the tablesaw sled. My sleds are lighter in weight and easier to use than the common sleds many craftsmen use, and I make them for a variety of specific uses, increasing the overall accuracy and efficiency of my work.

Sleds are much safer to use than traditional miter gauges. Many tablesaw injuries result from small offcuts being picked up and thrown by the blade; more serious injuries result from reaching into the blade to remove offcut stock. The natural motion of the sled into and then back away from the cut allows you to remove stock without putting your hands near the blade (**PHOTO A**). You will see a variety of sleds used in the course of this book, and despite some variations in their design, all start on common ground. The basics given here will remain true for all of the sleds used in this book.

The trickiest part of making a sled is installing the runners. They must be parallel to the blade and move smoothly in the miter-gauge slots on your saw table.

**SLEDS ARE SAFER** Sleds allow you to pull small parts safely away from the blade before removing them.

## Basic crosscut sled

This sled is both safer and more accurate than the miter gauge that comes with most tablesaws. It's also fast and easy to make.

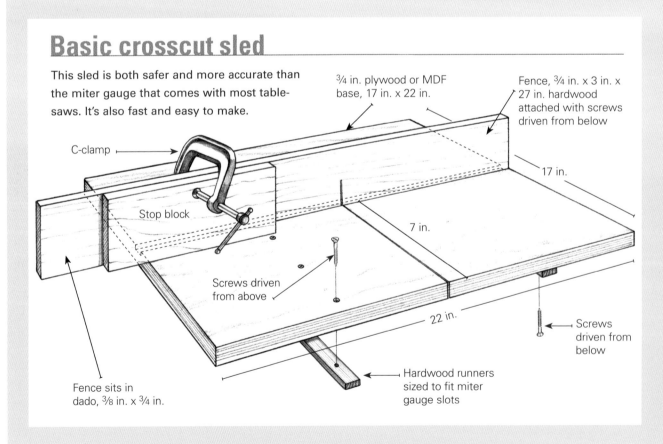

¾ in. plywood or MDF base, 17 in. x 22 in.

Fence, ¾ in. x 3 in. x 27 in. hardwood attached with screws driven from below

C-clamp

Stop block

17 in.

7 in.

Screws driven from above

22 in.

Screws driven from below

Fence sits in dado, ⅜ in. x ¾ in.

Hardwood runners sized to fit miter gauge slots

**1.** Start with a rectangular piece of plywood and two pieces of hardwood (one for the fence and another to form both runners). It helps if the plywood is square at all four corners, but this technique works as long as it has one straight edge.

**FIT THE FENCE TO THE BASE** Plane the fence stock to a thickness that fits snug in the dado. Alternately, you could widen the dado to fit already-planed stock.

**2.** Use a ¾-in.-wide dado blade in the tablesaw to make a dado cut ⅜ in. deep about 8 in. from the edge of the plywood. Plane the stock for the fence to fit in the dado. Alternately, you can widen the dado cut to accept the stock you're using for your fence. Aim for a fit that is snug **(PHOTO B)**.

**ATTACH THE RUNNER TO THE BASE** After milling the runner to fit in the miter-gauge slot, attach it to the base with a single screw. Square the runner to the back of the sled, then add screws down the length of the runner.

**3.** To make the runners, plane hardwood stock to fit the miter-guide slots in the tablesaw top.

**4.** Attach the first runner with a single screw and countersink it in place on the underside of the plywood base. Use a square to make certain that the runner is square to the edge you ran against the fence when you cut the dado. Holding the runner tightly in place, add two more screws **(PHOTO C)**.

**5.** Flip the sled base over and set the runner you just attached into the miter-gauge slot. Slide the second runner in place and use 1-in. drywall screws to attach it from above **(PHOTO D)**.

**6.** Attach the fence using 1⅝-in. screws driven in from the underside. Don't position any screws where they'll interfere with the path of the blade **(PHOTO E)**.

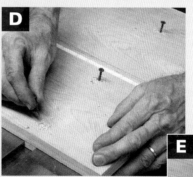

**ADD THE SECOND RUNNER** Fit the first sled runner into the tablesaw guide slot and place the second runner in the other slot. Use screws to attach the second runner from above.

**ATTACH THE FENCE** The fence is attached to the base using screws driven from underneath.

One of the best ways to hinge a tiny box is with hinge pins, but a high level of accuracy is required to get the best results. Whether you are planning to make one box or many, it's worthwhile to make a drilling guide for your drill press to accurately locate the pin holes in perfect alignment at each end of the box. This guide will accommodate boxes of various lengths while making minimal adjustments, so as to maintain accuracy.

Twelve-gauge copper wire is an easy source for pins of the right scale, and after stripping the wire it can be easily cut to whatever length you desire. The first thing you need to know about using 12-gauge copper wire is the appropriate hole size. I choose to use numbered drill bits; number 47 gives a tight fit on the wire where it passes deeply through the lid, and number 46, being slightly larger, gives a bit of clearance in the box ends for the lid to pivot with ease.

To build the drilling guide, use a piece of Baltic birch plywood secured to a hardwood base that you can clamp to the table of the drill press. I added a second piece of plywood as a back brace to make it rigid, and to be certain that it is held square. In addition, you will need to make an adjustable stop that can be clamped on either side of the box for drilling one side at a time. The end cap on the adjustable stop holds it square to the guide and parallel to the angle of the drill. A depth-support block is clamped in place to hold various lengths of box at the right height for drilling.

Use a brad-point bit in the drill press as you set up the guide. The tiny tip of the brad-point drill is much more accurate for measuring than a standard drill bit. I set the position of the drill bit so that it will be centered ⅛ in. from the back edge of the box, and carefully calculate the distance from the guide to the drill so that the pins will be properly positioned ⅛ in. from the underside of the lid. I use a business card as a spacer to provide clearance for the lid to rotate into an open position without rubbing on the body of the box. Once the distance from the bottom of the box to the hinge pin position has been set, the guide should remain in the same

position until the hinging is complete. The adjustable stop block, on the other hand, must be set first in a left-hand position, as shown on the facing page **(PHOTO A)**, and then moved to the right to drill the holes on the opposite end of the box and lid.

In order to get a good fit with the copper pins, first drill to the full depth of ⅝ in. using a number 47 drill bit **(PHOTO B)**. This hole will allow the pin to penetrate into the lid but will be too tight to rotate freely. After the preliminary holes are drilled on both ends of the box, drill shallower holes using a number 46 drill bit, which is only slightly larger than the 12-gauge copper wire.

Switching back and forth between different drill bits going to different depths and moving from one side to the other can be confusing, but the process is simplified by using set-up blocks of Baltic birch. Use a scrap piece of ⅛-in. Baltic birch as a set-up piece when installing the smaller drill bit that goes to a deeper

# Hinge pin drill guide

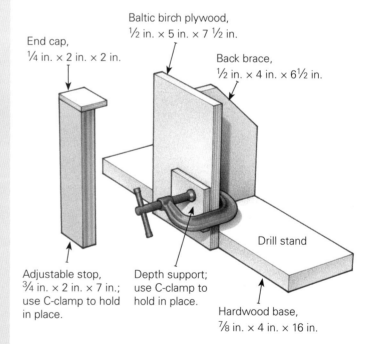

End cap,
¼ in. × 2 in. × 2 in.

Baltic birch plywood,
½ in. × 5 in. × 7 ½ in.

Back brace,
½ in. × 4 in. × 6½ in.

Drill stand

Adjustable stop,
¾ in. × 2 in. × 7 in.;
use C-clamp to hold
in place.

Depth support;
use C-clamp to
hold in place.

Hardwood base,
⅞ in. × 4 in. × 16 in.

depth (**PHOTO C**). Insert the drill bit loosely in the chuck and allow it to rest on the set-up piece as shown. Then tighten the chuck. When you are ready to drill with the larger bit to a shallower depth, add thickness to the set-up block by using an additional piece of ¼-in. Baltic birch placed on top. After the chuck is tightened on the larger bit, the depth it will penetrate will be reduced by ¼ in. The drill will only go ⅜ in. deep instead of the full depth, leaving plenty of stock in the lid to get a tight grip on the pins when they are tapped into place. The full set up is shown in the drawing on the facing page (**PHOTO D**).

**USE A STEEL RULE** and a brad-point bit to find the correct location for the hinge-pin holes.

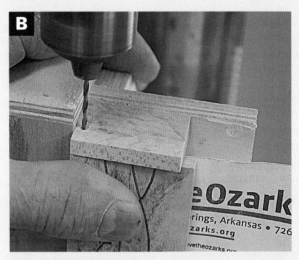

**HOLD THE LID** and box in position with a business card spacer between for the correct tolerance.

**A THIN PIECE OF SCRAP** helps to adjust the depth of the drill bit in the chuck.

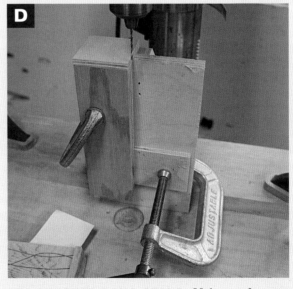

**THE FINISHED DRILL STAND.** Make one for your own drill press.

# Install the lid catch magnets

**A**

**DRILL THE HOLE** for the ⅛-in. magnet in the body of the box.

**B**

**I USE ⅛-IN. RARE EARTH MAGNETS INSTALLED** in the front of the box and lid to give the box a firm catch.

**1.** Drill with a ⅛-in. bit to a depth of ¹⁄₁₆ in. in the front edge of the body of the box. I use the fence to control the position of the hole (**PHOTO A**).

**2.** The fence makes drilling the matching hole for the lid easy, as it provides an exact location for the drill from the back of the box. You will need to shim the lid with another lid or a piece cut at the same angle to hold it at an angle 90 degrees to the drill. Re-adjust the depth of the drill to go only ¹⁄₁₆ in. into the stock (**PHOTO B**).

**DRILL THE MATCHING HOLE** for a magnet in the lid. Note that the fence position is the same for both parts but that the depth setting must be adjusted when fitting a magnet in the lid.

WORK
**SMART**

Don't install the magnets until you are ready for final assembly, as they can be difficult or impossible to remove.

**C**

USE WAX PAPER between the magnets as you glue them in place. Affixing one to the other as they are inserted in the lid and body of the box will help to make certain that they will attract and not repel.

**D**

CLOSING THE BOX with the wax paper in place will help double-check that the magnets are not reversed. The box would not close if they were.

**3.** Glue the rare earth magnets in place. If you have a very tight fit, common wood glue will work, but if your magnets are slightly loose, use epoxy. In either case, use wax paper between the magnets as you press them in place so that the glue will not stick your lid permanently in the closed position (**PHOTO C**). Make certain that the magnets in both the lid and body of the box are attracting each other and not forcing each other apart. Gluing them in with the wax paper between as shown will guarantee that their polarity is aligned to attract, because they will force the lid open if they are not (**PHOTO D**).

# Shape the box

**USE A DISK SANDER TO SHAPE THE FRONT** edge of the box. Because of the angled shape within the inlay, I chose an angular shape for the front of the box, but you can choose any shape you'd like.

USE A DISK SANDER to shape the front edge of the box. The angularity of the box complements the inlay design chosen for this box.

# A Meandering Veneer Patterned Box

Boxes with a meandering veneer pattern can be made in a variety of sizes and adapted to a variety of uses. But due to the expansion and contraction inherent in the use of solid woods and the conflict in grain direction where the ends are attached to the body of the box, I recommend that the stock used should not be over 2½ in. or 3 in. wide. This box, however, would be a great one to use other decorative techniques on. For instance, a simple technique using veneers could be used to make over a dozen boxes, which can be given as treasured gifts or even sold.

**1.** To make boxes with a meandering veneer pattern, as shown in the Salt and Pepper Shakers chapter (see p. 96), begin by making two curvy or meandering bandsaw cuts from one end of the lid stock to the other. These cuts should not cross. Then glue the hardwood back into a single block of wood with a layer of veneer inserted in each cut **(PHOTO A)**. As in making the salt and pepper shakers, the grain of the veneer must be at cross grain to the grain direction of the hardwood in order for it to bend around the curves cut in the wood. Choose contrasting veneer. Laying the veneer into the curved form requires careful alignment of the ends of the veneered stock to avoid gaps in the pattern or overlapping veneer, which would lead to a less secure joint.

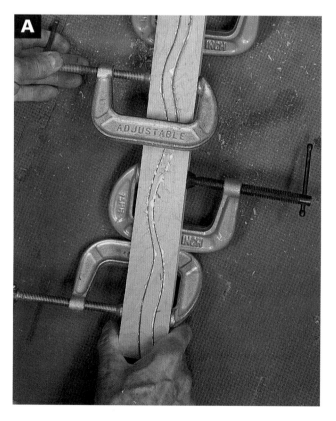

**MAKE LIDS** with embedded veneer lines by cutting stock and fitting it back together using veneer to fill the sawkerf formed by the bandsaw blade.

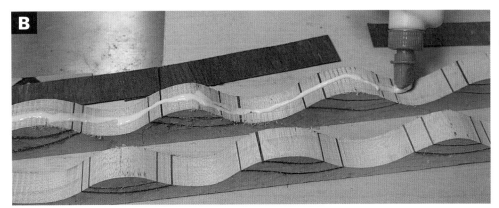

**CUT THE STOCK** again and spread glue for the second gluing operation.

**THE LIDS OF THESE BOXES** are ready for drilling pin holes. They have been left wide for shaping the front edge.

**AFTER THE LID STOCK** has been sawn into two pieces at a 7-degree angle, you will have lids for several boxes.

**2.** After the glue has set, make a third bandsaw cut from one end to the other and prepare veneers to fill the kerf. Apply glue to each surface and clamp just as before, being careful to align the edges of the stock **(PHOTO B )**. This two-step gluing operation can lead to stock for lids for a number of boxes.

**3.** Prepare stock for the other parts and assemble the body of the box just as you did to make the hinged pocket box in this chapter. This decorative technique with the meandering lines ensures that several boxes may be made and that each will be unique **(PHOTOS C & D )**.

**4.** Install the hinges temporarily as you shape the front edge, and install the magnets as a lid catch. The smooth curve at the front of the box reflects the sweeping curvature of the veneer pattern **(PHOTO E )**.

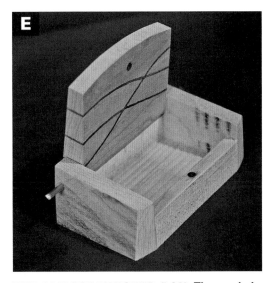

**THE ALMOST-FINISHED BOX.** The sanded curve at the front of the box complements the design of the lid stock embedded with veneer.

# A Sliding Pocket Box

This sliding pocket box is inspired by the small inlaid sliding-top boxes that are sold by Heartwood Creations. For longer than I've been a woodworker (I started in 1976), Heartwood Creations has sold small inlaid sliding-top boxes in gift stores throughout the United States and in other countries. My own effort is not to copy their boxes directly, but to make my own custom versions in a similar style. My versions of these boxes use tools and processes that are readily accessible to the home craftsman, and I make no claims that my techniques for making these boxes are at all similar to theirs. The fact that they make their boxes efficiently and at a fair price need not deter craftsmen from trying their hand at making similar boxes. You may never compete in quality or price with the fine boxes from Heartwood Creations, but you may still be able to make your own great little custom box and enjoy the process while doing so.

I offer two ways to form the inside of the box, so you can choose to make it with the router table or with the plunge router. In either case you will need to make a routing guide to control the cut.

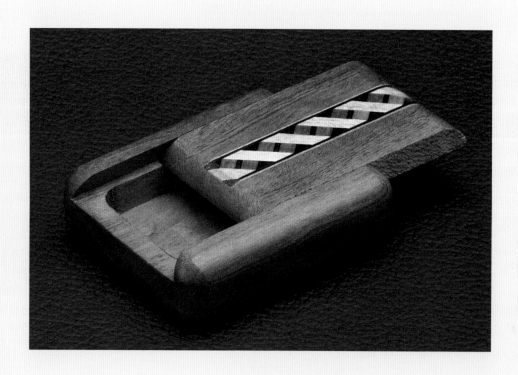

# Sliding pocket boxes

## Plunge router sliding pocket box

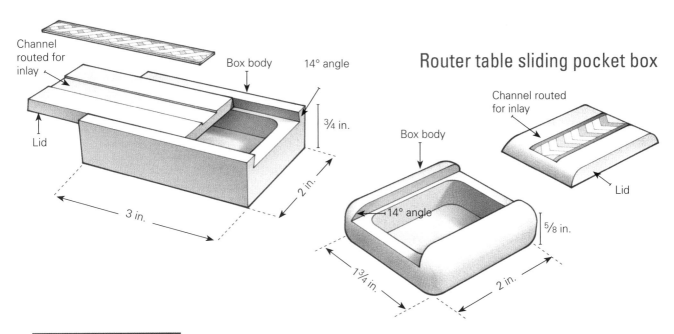

Channel routed for inlay

Lid

Box body

14° angle

¾ in.

2 in.

3 in.

## Router table sliding pocket box

Channel routed for inlay

Box body

Lid

14° angle

⅝ in.

1¾ in.

2 in.

## MATERIALS

| QUANTITY | PART | MATERIAL | SIZE | NOTES |
|---|---|---|---|---|
| **Router Table Sliding Pocket Box** | | | | |
| 1* | Body | Cherry or other hardwood | ⅝ in. x 1¾ in. x 2 in. | |
| 1 | Lid | Cherry or other hardwood | 3⁄16 in. x 1¼ in. x 2 in. | |
| 1 | Inlay | Commercial or shopmade | 2¼ in. per box | The inlay can be any size you choose. |
| **Plunge Router Sliding Pocket Box** | | | | |
| 1** | Body | Walnut or mahogany | ¾ in. x 2 in. x 3 in. | |
| 1 | Lid | Walnut or mahogany | 3⁄16 in. x 19⁄16 in. x 3 in. | |
| 1 | Inlay | Commercial or shopmade | 2¼ in. per box | The inlay can be any size you choose. |

*You may choose to make more than one box at a time.

**You'll probably want to make more than one version of this box at a time.

# Hollow the box using the router table

**TO HOLLOW THE INSIDE OF THE BOX USING** the router table, I build a framework that surrounds the router bit to confine the cut to the central area of the box. The cut must be done in increments to avoid taking too deep a cut at one time.

**A**

DRILL A ³⁄₈-IN.-DIAMETER HOLE **through the center of the set-up block.**

**1.** To make the router table guide, I start with a block of wood larger than the box I plan to make; it needs to be larger to accommodate travel room within the template. This set-up block is also useful in placing the guide accurately on the router table. I used a block 2½ in. by 3¼ in. and a ³⁄₈-in. straight-cut router bit. This block is perfectly sized for making a box 1¾ in. by 2 in. If you want to make a box of a different size from the one shown here, simply start with a different size block. Woodworkers should be cautioned, however, that this technique works best with tiny boxes. Due to expansion and contraction of wood, wide sliding dovetail lids as used here are hard to keep to a good fit in a larger box.

**2.** Find the center of the set-up block by marking diagonal lines from one corner to the other in each direction. Where the lines intersect, drill a hole through with a ³⁄₈-in. bit **(PHOTO A )**.

**B**

BUILD THE LOG-CABIN-LIKE ROUTER TABLE **guide around the set-up block using strips of ¼-in. Baltic birch plywood.**

# MAKE A ROUTER TABLE GUIDE

## Router table guide

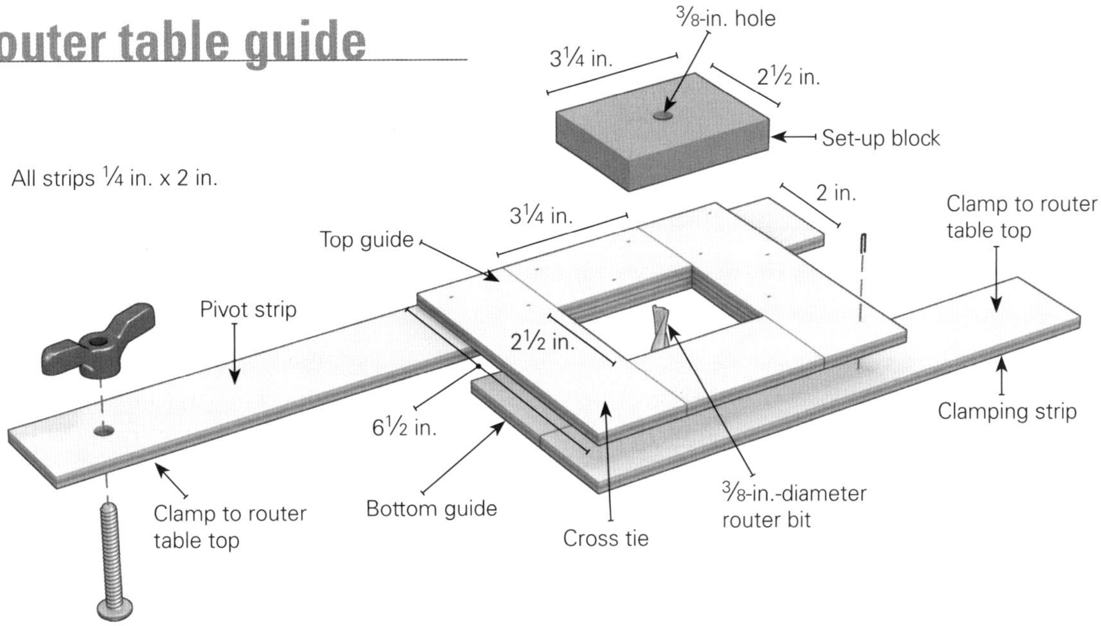

3/8-in. hole
3 1/4 in.
2 1/2 in.
Set-up block
All strips 1/4 in. x 2 in.
2 in.
3 1/4 in.
Clamp to router table top
Top guide
Pivot strip
2 1/2 in.
6 1/2 in.
Clamping strip
3/8-in.-diameter router bit
Clamp to router table top
Bottom guide
Cross tie


## MATERIALS

| QUANTITY | PART | MATERIAL | SIZE |
|---|---|---|---|
| 1 | Pivot strip | Baltic birch plywood | 1/4 in. x 2 in. x 17 1/2 in. |
| 2 | Cross ties | Baltic birch plywood | 1/4 in. x 2 in. x 6 1/2 in. |
| 1 | Clamping strip | Baltic birch plywood | 1/4 in. x 2 in. x 11 in. |
| 2 | Top guides | Baltic birch plywood | 1/4 in. x 2 in. x 3 1/4 in. |
| 2 | Bottom guides | Baltic birch plywood | 1/4 in. x 2 in. x 2 1/2 in. |
| 1 | Set-up block | Hardwood | 5/8 in. x 2 1/2 in. x 3 1/4 in. |

**3.** Cut strips of 1/4-in. Baltic birch and begin building a log-cabin-like structure around the set-up block. Two layers are essential so that the corners can overlap and provide structure, just as overlapping layers of a log cabin are used to build a strong house **(PHOTO B)** on the facing page. As shown in the illustration above, the end of one strip is drilled and affixed to the router table with a 3/8-in. carriage bolt that passes through the router table top and is secured with a plastic knob or nut. If your router table is not similarly equipped, simply drill a 3/8-in. hole in the top about 12 in.

**USE A BRAD NAILER** to tack the strips tightly around the set-up block.

or more from the bit and install a ⅜-in. carriage bolt through the top from underneath. The set-up block is positioned over the ⅜-in. router bit in the router table. Use a brad nailer and ⅜-in. brads to nail the pieces of Baltic birch tightly around the set-up block. The length of the ⅜-in. brads was chosen so that they would not protrude through the underside of the router table guide **(PHOTO C )**.

**4.** Use the carriage bolt to secure one end of the routing guide to the top of the router table and a C-clamp to secure the other. Remove the set-up block when both ends of the guide are held firmly in position **(PHOTO D )**.

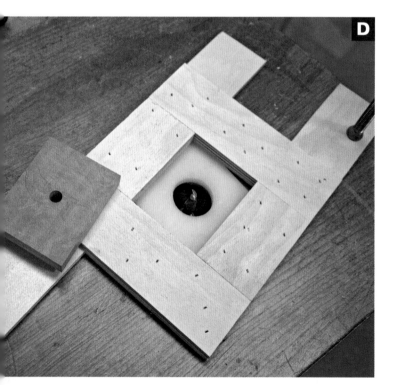

**AFTER THE ROUTER TABLE GUIDE is clamped firmly to the router table, remove the set-up block.**

A ⅜-in. hole drilled in the top of the router table allows for guides and pivot fences to be easily made and quickly added. Use a ⅜-in. carriage bolt and a nut or plastic knob to hold down one end and a C-clamp to secure the other.

**LOWER EACH BOX** into the cut and move it around until the first cut forms the inside shape of the box.

**5.** To rout the inside of the box, hold it tightly to one edge of the guide and lower it onto the spinning router bit. This must be done in a series of steps to reach the necessary depth, so you will need to raise the router bit in ⅛-in. increments **(PHOTO E )**. In order to keep a good grip on the box as the router extends higher above the table, I use hot-melt glue to attach guide blocks. These keep my fingers a safer distance from the bit **(PHOTO F )**.

**AS YOU ROUT DEEPER**, glued-on guide blocks give a more secure grip and keep your fingers at a greater distance from the cut.

# Form the dovetail channel

**ROUT THE DOVETAIL-SHAPED CHANNEL** in the top of the box where the sliding lid will fit.

**THE LID OF THIS BOX SLIDES INTO A** channel carefully shaped in the top of the box's body. Both the lid and the opening for the lid are formed with a 14-degree router bit designed for cutting dovetails in wood. The principle is simple. Once the dovetail-shaped opening is formed in the top of the box, the sliding dovetail shape on the lid allows it to slide within.

**1.** I use a 14-degree dovetail bit to hollow the channel for the sliding lid. Set the router bit to a height of $\frac{3}{16}$ in. and make a pass down the center of each box, using the fence to position the cut at the center of the stock. Then make additional passes after moving the fence farther from the bit **(PHOTO A )**.

**2.** Routing the channel for the lid is complete when the edge of the dovetail groove is equal or greater in width than the hole routed to form the interior of the box **(PHOTO B )**.

**WIDEN THE CUT** until the dovetail groove is equal or greater in width than the hole routed to form the interior of the box.

# Make the sliding lid

**I CUT THE SLIDING LID FROM LONGER STOCK** to make handling it safe. I use the same 14-degree router bit for this operation as was used to form the dovetail channel in the top, so that the angle will be the same. As an alternative, the same operation can be done on the tablesaw, cutting one side and then the other at a 14-degree angle. Whether using the tablesaw or router table, you will want to sneak up on a perfect fit by moving the fence in small increments, using trial and error. Note that on the router table, I pass the stock between the router bit and fence **(PHOTO A )**. In order for this operation to be done safely, the stock should be moved from the left to the right—not the usual direction. If moved from the right to the left, the router bit will pull the stock into the cut. Also, this operation must be done with a guard in place, as shown below **(PHOTO B )**. You will know when you have a perfect fit by testing the lid in the box. It should slide with a bit of effort and not with such ease that it will fall out of the box **(PHOTO C )**.

**SET UP THE ROUTER** to form the sliding lid. Router height should be equal to or greater than the thickness of the stock.

**CLAMP A GUARD** over the router bit and rout from left to right.

**WITH TRIAL AND ERROR** you will arrive at a perfect fit.

# Hollow the box using the plunge router

**THIS TECHNIQUE DIFFERS FROM THE ROUTER** table technique in that the plunge router with a template-following router bit is lowered into the stock in increments of ⅛ in. or so. Also, instead of cutting the boxes to length first, the routing is done on a longer piece and the boxes are cut to length after the interiors are formed.

**1.** Decide on the interior dimensions of the box and build your template equal to that size. A box 2 in. by 3 in. with an interior space of 1⅜ in. by 2⅜ in. requires a plunge router guide with an opening size of 1⅜ in. by 2⅜ in. and blocking on the underside to position the 2-in. by 3-in. stock so that it is in the center of your guide.

**2.** I use ¼-in. Baltic birch plywood to build the plunge router guide log-cabin style, as was done for the router table guide. Use a brad nailer with ⅜-in.-long brads to nail the corners and form the template in two layers. Overlapping corners are the key to its strength **(PHOTO A )**.

**3.** When the upper part of the guide is complete, add positioning strips on the underside that will hold the workpiece in position for routing. As you install these strips they should be held tightly against your working stock and spaced so it will be held in the exact center of the guide **(PHOTO B )**.

**USE A BRAD NAILER** to build a plunge router guide.

**ATTACH STRIPS** to the underside of the guide. These will be used to position the stock.

## Plunge router guide

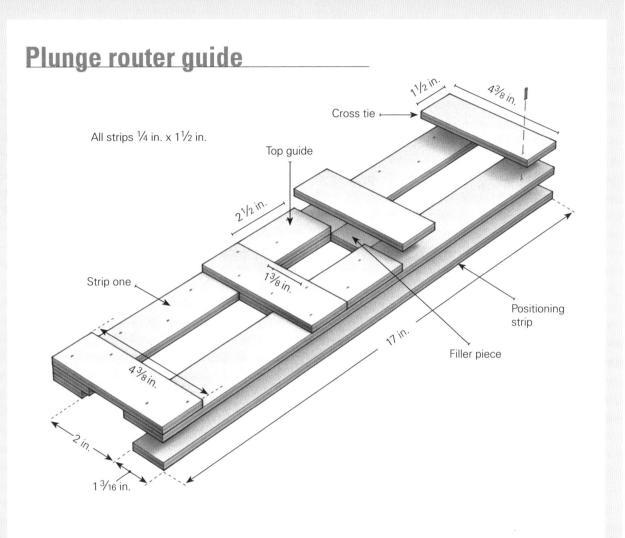

All strips ¼ in. x 1½ in.

Cross tie

1½ in.

4⅜ in.

Top guide

2½ in.

Strip one

1⅜ in.

4⅜ in.

17 in.

Positioning strip

Filler piece

2 in.

1³⁄₁₆ in.

## MATERIALS

| QUANTITY | PART | MATERIAL | SIZE |
|---|---|---|---|
| 2 | Strip ones | Baltic birch plywood | ¼ in. x 1½ in. x 17 in. |
| 4 | Cross ties | Baltic birch plywood | ¼ in. x 1½ in. x 4⅜ in. |
| 2 | Top guides | Baltic birch plywood | ¼ in. x 1½ in. x 2½ in. |
| 2 | Positioning strips | Baltic birch plywood | ¼ in. x 1³⁄₁₆ in. x 17 in. |
| 2 | Filler pieces | Baltic birch plywood | ¼ in. x 1½ in. x 1⅜ in. |

A TEMPLATE-FOLLOWING ROUTER BIT and shopmade routing guide are perfect box-making companions.

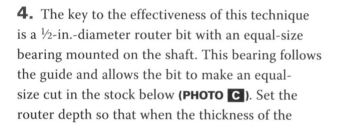

SET THE DEPTH OF CUT about ⅛ in. less than the thickness of the guide and stock.

**4.** The key to the effectiveness of this technique is a ½-in.-diameter router bit with an equal-size bearing mounted on the shaft. This bearing follows the guide and allows the bit to make an equal-size cut in the stock below (**PHOTO C**). Set the router depth so that when the thickness of the

box and two thicknesses of Baltic birch plywood are stacked on the router base, about ⅛ in. of plywood remains above the full depth of the cut (**PHOTO D**).

**5.** Clamp both the workpiece and the guide firmly to the top of the workbench, then use the plunge router to remove stock in increments of about ⅛ in. or less. Plunge the router bit in at the center and work your way to the outside, then plunge in for a deeper cut (**PHOTO E**). The stops set on the router will keep it from plunging in too deep.

**6.** Move the workpiece to a new position to rout more boxes from the same length of stock (**PHOTO F**).

**7.** As with the router table version of the box, use the router table with a 14-degree dovetail bit to rout a channel for the sliding lid (**PHOTO G**).

PLUNGE AND ROUT. Stop when you have reached full depth.

**THESE BOXES HAVE BEEN ROUTED** and are now ready to cut to length.

**ROUT THE CHANNEL** for the sliding lid.

# Create your own inlay

**YOU COULD USE COMMERCIAL INLAY** banding, as the Heartwood Creation boxes do, but I am more inclined to make patterns of my own for a couple of reasons. One is that I like showcasing the beauty of our local woods. Second, whereas my patterns are usually not as complex as commercially made inlay, I can take pride in having made them myself. I can start a pattern by simply gluing together strips of wood, and then playing with the process of cutting apart and reassembling what I glued up in the first place.

**1.** Glue strips of multicolored hardwoods of various thicknesses between cauls. Apply enough clamping pressure that some glue appears on the outside of the assembled strips **(PHOTO A )**.

**BUILD A BLOCK** of raw material for crafting inlay from strips of multicolored hardwoods.

CUT THE BLOCK in pieces at a 22½-degree angle.

CAREFULLY ARRANGE and glue the pieces into a new block.

**2.** Flatten one side of your glued-up block on the jointer, and then use the miter saw to cut short pieces. Flip the strips in relation to each other as they are cut (**PHOTO B**). Here I have used a 22½-degree angle for each cut.

**3.** Line the cut strips up on a board and apply glue between each piece (**PHOTO C**). Keep them carefully aligned as you apply clamping pressure (**PHOTO D**).

**4.** After the glue has dried, square the edges and flatten one face on the jointer, then use a thin-kerf ripping blade on the tablesaw to cut the assembled block into thin strips (³⁄₆₄ in. to ⅛ in. thick) (**PHOTO E**).

**5.** Cut the inlay you plan to use from the wider strip, and then cut it to the width you want to inlay in the lid (**PHOTO F**).

**USE CLAMPS** to keep the pieces tight, flat, and secure until the glue sets.

**USE A THIN-KERF BLADE** on the tablesaw to rip the block into thin strips.

**CUT A PIECE FROM THE INLAY STOCK** to fit the lid. You will have plenty left over for other interesting projects.

# Inlay the lid

ROUT THE LIDS for the inlay to fit. Here I'm using both commercial and shopmade inlays.

YOU MAY FIND a block plane useful for reaching a perfect fit, as there may be some variation in the width of the inlay strips.

USE C-CLAMPS and cauls to hold the inlay in place as the glue dries.

**YOU CAN INLAY THE SLIDING LID WITH** either store-bought or shopmade inlay.

**1.** To groove the sliding lid for the inlay to fit, I use a small straight-cut router bit with its height set at just $\frac{1}{64}$ in. less than the thickness of the inlay. Use the fence to control the position of the cut. You may center the cut in the sliding lid, or offset it for a more dramatic effect. Widen the space between the fence and router bit to widen the channel until the inlay fits **(PHOTO A )**.

**2.** Carefully fit the inlay, either by widening the channel or by lightly planing or sanding the strips for a perfect fit **(PHOTO B )**.

**3.** When you have achieved a perfect fit, spread glue in the routed channel and insert the inlay strips. Use clamps and cauls to exert pressure until the glue sets **(PHOTO C )**.

**4.** After the inlay is completely installed, cut the lid to length on the miter saw, or on the tablesaw with a sled. In either case, use a stop block to control the length of the cut and a pencil with an eraser end to control the stock while keeping your hands a safe distance from the blade **(PHOTO D )**.

USE THE MITER SAW or the sled on the tablesaw to cut the lid stock to finished length.

# Sand and rout the pocket box

**1.** A flat sheet of sandpaper laid on a flat surface is sufficient to flatten the inlay so that it is flush with the surface of the box, though some craftsmen would prefer a power tool approach with a belt sander. In either case, sand the topside flush and sand the ends so they are equal in length to the box.

**2.** Use a ³⁄₁₆-in.-radius or ¼-in.-radius roundover bit in the router table to round the corners and edges of the box **(PHOTO A)**.

**3.** I often use a random-orbit sander held upside down to sand the edges of small boxes. The advantage of this device is that instead of holding a large sander, I hold the box instead **(PHOTO B)**. On the other hand, you would be amazed at the efficiency of hand sanding a tiny box. Use self-adhesive sandpaper mounted to a flat piece of MDF, and drag the corners across to remove burn marks from the router and to achieve a smooth finish **(PHOTO C)**. Sand through 180-grit, 240-grit, and 320-grit before applying a Danish oil finish to bring the colors of the wood to life.

**ROUND THE CORNERS** and edges of the box with a roundover bit in the router table.

**SAND THE BOXES** with a random-orbit sander.

**OR TRY YOUR HAND** at hand sanding. Self-adhesive sandpaper on a flat surface helps.

WORK **SMART**

After finishing, use a bit of paste wax on the edges and tracks of sliding lids to help them move smoothly in the grooves.

# A Bentwood Box

S ome woods bend naturally, whereas others are brittle and snap. But if steamed or soaked in boiling water, wood becomes much more flexible, and if bent to a particular shape and allowed to fully dry, it will hold its new shape, enabling you to make some beautifully shaped boxes. There is a long tradition of making bentwood boxes in many cultures, and beautiful examples of these can be found all around the world.

My own interest in bentwood boxes is in part a result of my Norwegian heritage. In Norway, a box like this one (though they are rarely this small) would be called a *tine* (pronounced "teen-a"), meaning cheese box, because of the traditional use of bentwood boxes in the making of cheese. I prefer to call these boxes "bentwood beauties," for they are a wonderful expression of tiny craftsmanship. Due to the process through which

they are made, no two will ever be quite alike.

I chose to make this box from elm, which is well known as a wood suitable for bending. Other fine woods can be used. For instance, cherry, walnut, maple, oak, ash, hickory, and many other North American hardwoods could be used in place of the elm, but you will find that cherry and maple are slightly more brittle and likely to break during the process.

When it comes to making a lid for this box, you can expand your wood selection even further. I used a scrap of olive burl wood to make the lid for this box and used crotch-figured walnut for others shown at the end of the chapter. One great thing about the process used to make this box is that one bending operation can yield more than one box. Another is that it can be done on a hot plate or on the stove in your kitchen using nothing more than a pot of boiling water to bring the wood up to bending temperature.

# Bentwood box

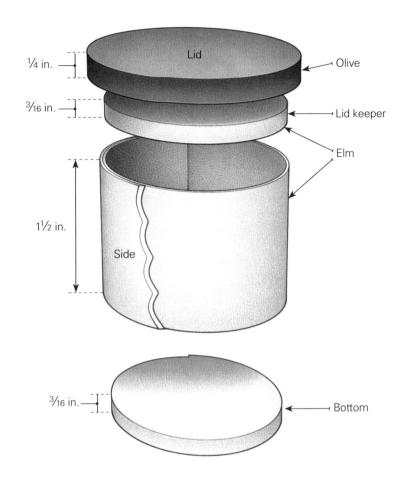

1/4 in.

Lid

Olive

3/16 in.

Lid keeper

Elm

1 1/2 in.

Side

3/16 in.

Bottom

## MATERIALS

| QUANTITY | PART | MATERIAL | SIZE | NOTES |
|---|---|---|---|---|
| 1 | Side* | Elm | 1/16 in. or less x 1 1/2 in. x 7 in.* | |
| 1 | Bottom | Elm | Cut from stock 3/16 in. x 1 1/2 in. | |
| 1 | Lid keeper | Elm | Cut from stock 3/16 in. x 1 1/2 in. | |
| 1 | Lid | Olive | Cut from stock 1/4 in. x 1 3/4 in. | |
| 6 | Tacks (optional) | Copper | 2 1/4 in. | from John Wilson (www.shakerovalbox.com) |

*For safety, rip stock in 21-in. to 24-in. lengths. Up to three boxes can be formed at a time from this length.

# Prepare your stock

**HOW THICK YOU CUT YOUR WOOD MAY** require a bit of experimentation.

**1.** I started with rough lumber and ripped it on the saw to about 1⅝ in. wide. I then flattened one face on the jointer so the first slice would come out useful and true.

**2.** I cut the elm for this box into thin slices slightly less than ¹⁄₁₆ in. thick. It is important to use a zero-clearance insert in the saw to fully support the stock. It is equally important to work with stock long enough to guide it safely through the cut. It takes about 8 in. of stock to make a box 1½ in. by 2 in. In other words, from a piece of wood 24 in. long, you can expect to make three boxes, and by doing so, you will have stock that is safer to handle through the cut.

# Boil and bend the wood

**1.** To test if your wood is ready for bending, coil it to fit in a pot. If it breaks, it is best to rip another piece a bit thinner on the saw. If you can't get it to coil easily to fit the pot, you may want to choose another wood **(PHOTO A )**.

**2.** Heat the water in your pot to a rolling boil and then put the roll of wood in. Cover with the lid for about 10 to 15 minutes of steady boil **(PHOTO B )**.

**USE A TWIST TIE** or bent wire to hold the thin wood in a roll small enough to fit inside your pot.

**WHEN THE WATER BOILS,** put the roll of wood in and put the cover back on as the water returns to a boil.

**3.** To begin bending the wood, simply remove it from the water using kitchen tongs and roll it around a large dowel. The one I use is 1½ in. in diameter, though any cylindrical form, like a piece of PVC pipe, will work also. Wear gloves to protect your hands from the heat **(PHOTO C )**.

**4.** After rolling the bent stock tightly around the dowel, pull the dowel out from the center of the roll and use a clamp to squeeze the roll into an oval shape. If you've followed my suggestions and used a long piece of stock, you can make a box from every 8 in. or 9 in. of rolled stock and in a range of small sizes, with the smallest coming from the center of the roll. Wait until the wood has fully dried to cut it into individual box forms **(PHOTO D )**.

   The most difficult part of making this box is waiting for the stock to dry sufficiently for the next step. You can tell if the wood is still slightly damp because it will feel noticeably cool to the touch. Be patient. It will take at least two or three days for the wood to dry fully in its new shape.

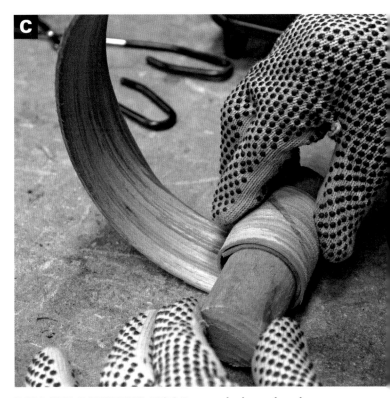

ROLL THE SOFTENED WOOD around a large dowel.

## WORK SMART

It is difficult to roll a single box and there are safety advantages to working with longer stock. I therefore work with stock 21 in. to 24 in. long to make this box, and then I can create up to three boxes at once.

AFTER REMOVING THE DOWEL from the center of the roll, use a clamp to force it into an oval shape.

# Assemble the box

**1.** To turn the rolled stock into boxes, begin unrolling one end and cut enough from it to form a box. There must be some overlap of the sides in order to have a place to glue the shape into a box. You can use sharp scissors, a saw, or a knife to cut the boxes from the roll **(PHOTO A)**. The exact amount of overlap is not critical to the useful beauty of the finished box **(PHOTO B)**.

**2.** You can leave the outside edge plain or you can do some decorative carving. I used a carving knife and a sandpaper-wrapped dowel to shape the outside end of the box, as shown below **(PHOTO C)**. Other options are shown at the end of the chapter (see p. 60).

**USE SCISSORS,** a knife, or a small handsaw to cut the roll into the box shape.

**FROM A 16-IN.-LONG PIECE OF WOOD** you can make two boxes.

**SHAPE THE END** that will overlap at the front of the box. I used a carving knife and sanding stick to carve this design.

**3.** Prior to gluing the box into its final form, sand the surface where the two ends of the strip of wood overlap. To do this, bend the shaped wood back far enough that you can reverse which end is on the outside. This will make that surface available to sand smooth with a sanding block **(PHOTO D )**.

**4.** Apply glue to the sanded surface, but be careful to get glue only on the area that the outside end of the box will cover. To make clamping quick and easy, I use Nexabond™ CA glue, which dries clear and very quickly **(PHOTO E )**.

**5.** After applying the glue, uncoil and recoil the box into its finished shape and use clamps to hold the ends down tight. With this glue, clamping only a few minutes is sufficient **(PHOTO F )**.

**TO PREPARE FOR SANDING, pry the box open slightly so that the outside end can be moved to the inside.**

**AFTER SANDING, apply glue where the end will overlap the sides. I use Nexabond CA glue for a rapid cure.**

**USE CLAMPS TO PULL the ends of the box into position and leave them on for a few minutes.**

# Make a bottom and a lid keeper

TRACE THE INSIDE SHAPE of the top and bottom of the box on ³⁄₁₆-in.-thick elm stock.

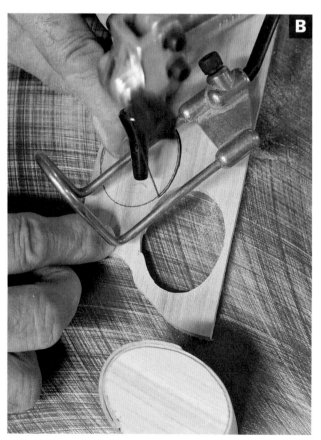

USE A SCROLLSAW to cut the bottom and top to fit inside the box sides.

**1.** I use a scrollsaw to cut a piece of elm for the bottom and top of the box. Use a pencil to trace around the inside of the box while it is held tightly to the stock. At left **(PHOTO A )**, I've traced around the inside at both the bottom and top edges of the box. The piece traced at the top will become the lid keeper and will be glued to the underside of the lid to keep it in place.

**2.** Use a scrollsaw to cut around one part and then the other. To get a tight fit, I try to keep the blade just barely outside the pencil line **(PHOTO B )**.

**3.** If you've done a perfect job, the pieces will fit without sanding. If not, the bottom and lid keeper may quickly be shaped to a better fit by using a sanding block on the edge. The bottom should fit reasonably tight. How tight the lid keeper should fit is a matter for your own judgment. I want it to fit tight enough that the box will not fall open in error **(PHOTO C )**. When testing the fit of your bottom and lid keeper, do not put them both in at the same time, as you may have difficulty getting them out before the lid is shaped and glued in place.

**4.** Glue the lid keeper to the piece of decorative or contrasting hardwood that will serve as your lid. Be dead certain that the side with the pencil marking is on the outside and is not facing the piece for the lid. If not, you've just glued your keeper inside out and the lid will not fit the box. Be careful, too, to keep your box bottom in place so you don't get them mixed up **(PHOTO D )**.

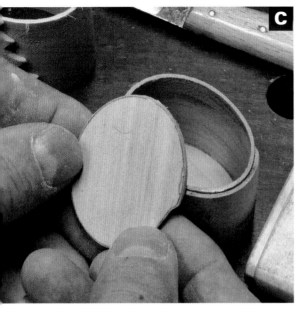

AS YOU FIT THE LID KEEPER and bottom, some sanding may be required.

GLUE THE LID KEEPER to a piece of figured hardwood.

# Shape the lid

**FOR THIS TINY BOX, I WANTED THE LID TO** overhang the sides slightly to make it easy to lift off without a knob.

**1.** With the lid keeper glued to the lid stock and the body of the box fitted to the keeper, use a rubber band or string to provide a consistent space between the pencil line and the body of the box while you trace the lid **(PHOTO A )**.

**2.** Use a scrollsaw to cut along the outside edge of the line you just marked. Use a sanding block to smooth the edge. This lid will overlap uniformly on all sides and will be easy to grasp when opening the box **(PHOTO B )**.

USE A SPACER as you trace around the edges of the box sides to create a cutline for the lid. I used a rubber band as my spacer.

USE THE SCROLLSAW to shape the lid.

**NO TWO BENTWOOD BEAUTIES** need be alike. Vary the design of the overlap in the front, use contrasting woods, and experiment with the lid shape.

Every bentwood box you make will come out differently from the last. This may be simply the result of choosing a different wood to start with, or because you've coiled the wood tighter during construction. Variations in design are inherent in the process through which they are made.

If you make them as I do, by coiling up a strip long enough to make three or even four boxes, they will differ in size, and might even be able to nest within each other. In the example at right I started with a strip of wood about 30 in. long and I was able to create four boxes by cutting them apart using the scrollsaw. I simply worked the blade into the coil of wood to cut through layers at the point where there was sufficient overlap to form a box. After making three cuts, I'm left with four boxes from a single bending operation **(PHOTO A )**.

**A SINGLE COIL OF BENT WOOD** can make as many as three or four boxes, depending on the length of stock and how tightly you wrap it.

**A SMOOTHLY SHAPED PIECE** of figured walnut makes a nice contrasting lid.

**THE SHAPE OF THE LID** can follow the shape of the body of the box. Here the loose end inspires the lid shape.

Besides creating boxes of various sizes, you may choose to vary your lid design. Use a different contrasting wood for the lid or angle the lid in one way or another. A simple dome-shaped lid of figured walnut looks good **(PHOTO B)**. You may even want to alter the lid's shape; allowing it to run wild following a loose end on the box itself **(PHOTO C)**.

Another way to vary the look of your box is to add embellishment. Use copper tacks to clinch the ends of the stock or to attach the bottom. Small touches like this are a great way to add interest to your box **(PHOTO D)**.

**COPPER TACKS CAN BE USED** to strengthen the attachment of the end and bottom; here they also give the box a Shaker look.

# An Heirloom
# Lift-Lid Box

O ne relatively easy way to make a box more interesting is to shape its sides using a molding cutter in the router table. Boxes with molded sides can be made in a variety of sizes, though it can be a challenge to decide which molding cutter to use for various box sizes. The molding cutter used on this box is intended to duplicate common antique molding plane patterns, but it would take several different planes and a great deal of steady labor to achieve the results that a router can get in minutes. Best of all, it is just the right size to make a lovely tiny box.

Because of the small size of this box, glued miter joints are sufficient to hold the parts together for generations. The Baltic birch bottom panel, glued into grooves in the box sides, gives additional strength and longevity to the box. And a simple lift lid provides ready access to whatever treasures you keep inside.

You can use a combination of bits to achieve a variety of molding shapes. And you may enjoy a bit of play in this area. For instance, in the Design Options at the end of this chapter I use a furniture-maker bit that is designed to make a smooth curve, in combination with a double roundover bit to make a box with an Asian design motif. Flipped over upside down, this same molding could be used to make a tiny box with a more modern Scandinavian look. With any of these beautiful small boxes, a hand-turned wooden knob (see p. 110 and p. 120) or a commercially made brass knob would be the perfect complement.

# Heirloom lift-lid box

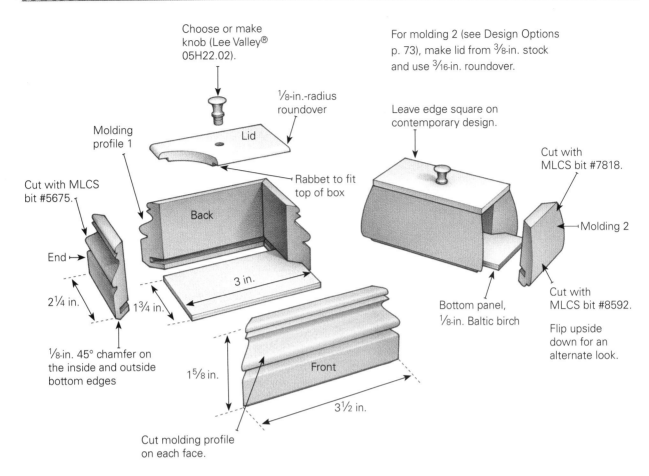

Choose or make knob (Lee Valley® 05H22.02).

For molding 2 (see Design Options p. 73), make lid from ³⁄₈-in. stock and use ³⁄₁₆-in. roundover.

Molding profile 1

¹⁄₈-in.-radius roundover

Lid

Leave edge square on contemporary design.

Cut with MLCS bit #7818.

Cut with MLCS bit #5675.

Rabbet to fit top of box

Back

Molding 2

End

3 in.

2¹⁄₄ in.

1³⁄₄ in.

Cut with MLCS bit #8592.

Bottom panel, ¹⁄₈-in. Baltic birch

¹⁄₈-in. 45° chamfer on the inside and outside bottom edges

1⁵⁄₈ in.

Front

Flip upside down for an alternate look.

3¹⁄₂ in.

Cut molding profile on each face.

## MATERIALS

| QUANTITY | PART | MATERIAL | SIZE | NOTES |
|---|---|---|---|---|
| 2 | Front and back* | Sycamore | ¹⁄₂ in. x 1⁵⁄₈ in. x 3¹⁄₂ in. | |
| 2 | Ends* | Sycamore | ¹⁄₂ in. x 1⁵⁄₈ in. x 2¹⁄₄ in. | |
| 1 | Bottom panel | Baltic birch | ¹⁄₈ in. x 1³⁄₄ in. x 3 in. | |
| 1 | Lid | Spalted maple | **¹⁄₄ in. x 1¹¹⁄₁₆ in. x 2¹⁵⁄₁₆ in. | |
| 1 | Knob | Brass | | www.LeeValley.com, stock number 05H22.02 |

*The front, back, and ends are all cut from one piece of molding ¹⁄₂ in. x 1⁵⁄₈ in. x 13 in.
** The lid for the box in the Design Options section is made from ³⁄₈-in. stock.

# Make the molding

**MAKE YOUR FIRST MOLDING CUT** with the bearing set slightly in from the face of the fence so it does not cut full depth.

**A SECOND PASS** completes the molding. A large push block ensures a secure and safe cut.

**CUT THE GROOVE** for the bottom panel.

**I MAKE THE MOLDING FOR THE SIDES OF** this box on the router table using a close-fitting pivot fence that you can easily make in your own shop. The close fit of the router bit in the fence keeps long strands of fiber from being torn off from the stock. I work with a long piece of stock for the front, back, and ends and cut it to length in a later step.

**1.** The molding for this box is formed with the stock in an upside-down position and the height of the router bit set so that a round bead is formed on what will be the top edge of the body of the box. I make the molding in a two-step process. First cut with the bearing of the router bit set about 1/16 in. inside the fence. Normally the guide bearing on a router bit should be set flush with the fence, but doing this operation in two steps gives cleaner results. Make your first pass, with the bearing set in slightly from the surface of the fence, using a push block to safely apply pressure against the fence and guide the molding stock through the cut (**PHOTO A**).

**2.** Bring the bearing flush to the fence for the second pass. This will give a cleaner cut than trying to remove all the stock at the same time (**PHOTO B**). Note how the push block is long enough to support nearly the full length of the stock, so that it can be held tightly against the fence throughout its length.

**3.** Use the tablesaw to make a cut down the length of the stock to fit the bottom panel. I set the blade height at 1/4 in. and set the fence so that the Baltic birch bottom panel will fit 1/8 in. from the bottom of the box (**PHOTO C**).

One of the things in my shop that gets the most attention from students and visitors is my simple router table. It's nothing more than a piece of plywood with a router base mounted to the underside that can be clamped to any workbench and put away when the routing operation is complete. Whereas many craftsmen spend big bucks on large router tables, or spend many hours making one, mine was quickly made, was put to use less than an hour from conception, and has lasted over 25 years despite regular use.

Part of what makes this router table so useful is its equally simple pivot fence. Or to be more precise, I should say, "pivot fences," for I've made many of them. The pivot fence is mounted to the top of the router table by a ⅜-in. carriage bolt and a plastic knob at the pivoting end, and is held in place by a C-clamp at the other. This simple approach allows me to make fences in even less time than the router table took in the first place and leaves me much more time for boxmaking. You will see a fence in its most simple form on

the bottom of p. 69. In this case a hole is drilled in a board to provide the clearance needed for the pilot bearing to align with the fence. The same fence can be flipped over when the hole is not needed.

To make the molding fence, I first drilled a ⅜-in. hole in the piece of 2-in.-square hardwood I'm using to make my fence in order to attach it to the router table top with a carriage bolt. After carefully measuring the distance from the carriage bolt to the center of the router bit, I marked that same distance on the stock for the fence and drilled a ½-in. hole with a Forstner bit along one edge. The hole does not need to be drilled all the way through but does need to be drilled deep enough that when the fence is pivoted into the spinning router bit the bit can cut its own profile into the side, as shown above. This hole is needed to allow the bearing to be flush with the surface of the fence. Use a clamp at one corner to secure the router table to the workbench and a C-clamp to secure the fence to the router table (as shown below).

**CLOSE PROFILE FENCE helps to prevent tearout of long strips during molding making.**

An additional advantage of this router table is that you can add a zero-clearance feature to each change of router bit. This will reduce the size of the opening in the router table to correspond perfectly to the size of the router bit being used. This is shown in use in the Japanese Puzzle Box chapter. Simply drill a ⅜-in. hole in a piece of ⅛-in. Baltic birch and clamp it down under the router table fence. When the router bit cuts into it, it provides zero clearance on the cut.

**THE FENCE PIVOTS on a ⅜-in. carriage bolt at one end and clamps firmly at the other.**

# Cut miters on a tablesaw

**YOU CAN MITER THE CORNERS AND CUT** the box sides to length using the tablesaw.

**1.** I use a 45-degree sled because it is one of the safest and most accurate ways to cut miters at the ends of box parts. Make a trim cut at 45 degrees at one end of the stock (**PHOTO A**).

**2.** Flip the stock over against the stop block to cut the miter at the other end and to cut the part to the correct length. The stop block should be set so that the long parts of the box front and back will be 3½ in. long. In order to cut the ends of the box shorter, I also use a spacer block cut 1¼ in. wide to offset the difference in length between the two parts. The photo below (**PHOTO B**) shows two important things. One, the stop block clamped to the sled is wide enough to match the full width of the molding stock and touch at the longest point. Two, I use a hold-down stick to hold the stock while keeping my fingers a safe distance from the blade.

**CUT THE FIRST MITER** on the tablesaw face side down.

Even the small width of a pencil line can make the difference between sloppy work and perfectly fitted joints. By using guides, sleds, and stop blocks you can alleviate the errors easily. Rather than risk inaccuracies from marking on stock with a pencil or knife and then aligning it with the sawblade, simply measure from the edge of the sawblade to the stop block.

**CUT THE SECOND MITER** with the face side of the stock up. A shopmade hold-down keeps my hands away from the blade.

**3.** To cut the next adjoining part, trim the miter at one end, as in step 1 **(PHOTO C )**.

**4.** Use a spacer block between the stop block and workpiece to cut a shorter piece for the box end **(PHOTO D )**. Make a box with matching corners by moving back and forth, using the spacer block between alternating parts.

**EACH PIECE REQUIRES** a 45-degree trimming cut at one end before cutting the miter at the other.

**USE A SPACER BLOCK** when cutting every other part.

# Cut miters on a compound miter saw

**YOU CAN ALSO USE A COMPOUND MITER** saw to cut the parts for this box, but I advise reading the safety instructions in the sidebar on p. 19 for additional guidance.

**1.** Begin by cutting your parts to length; I cut the parts about ¼ in. longer than is required for their final length. Mark the length on the miter saw backing board and begin with square cuts. (Note the pencil lines marked on the fence for initial length **(PHOTO A )**.

**2.** I align the stock with one mark and then the other as I alternate between parts of different lengths **(PHOTO B )**. Make sure the saw is allowed to come to a complete stop while in the down position to ensure a safe and clean cut **(PHOTO C )**.

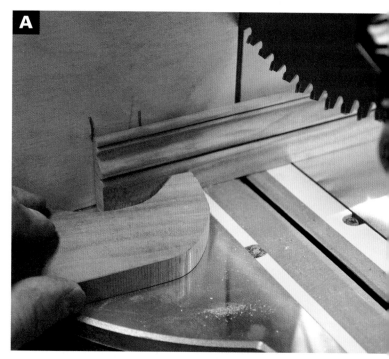

TRIM THE PARTS to initial length, making square cuts. The pencil marks on the fence provide the locations for alternating cuts, long for the front and back pieces and short for the end pieces.

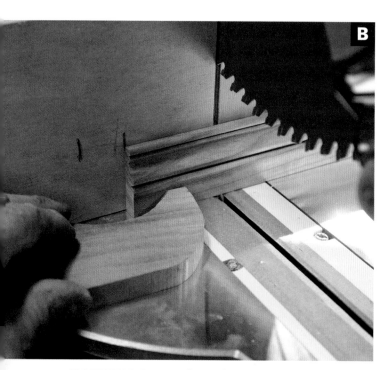

MAKE THE CUTS using a shopmade hold-down to keep your hands a safe distance from the blade.

STOP THE SAW with the blade in the down position for a safer and more accurate cut.

**3.** Tilt the saw to a 45-degree angle to make the miter cuts. Position the stop block on the side where the rotation of the blade will be pushing the stock toward the stop block **(PHOTO D)**. Note the use of shopmade hold-downs to keep hands a safe distance from the blade.

**4.** Make your cuts on one end and then the other of each part. The stop block will have to be moved between cuts, or a spacer block can be used, as in cutting the miters on the tablesaw **(PHOTO E)**.

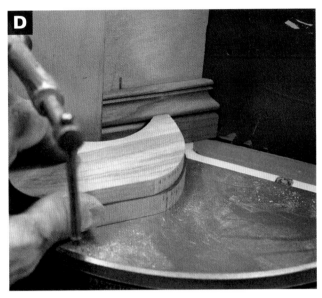

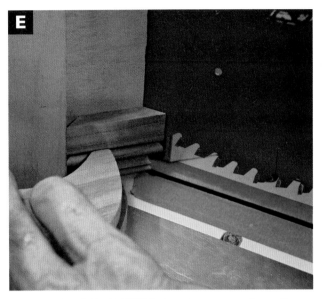

**CUT THE MITERS** with the sawblade angled away from the stop block, to provide clearance for the hold-down and stop block and so the blade's action pulls toward the stop block.

**USE TWO HOLD-DOWNS** to get a secure grip on the uneven molded stock.

# Assemble the box

**1.** After the miters have been cut, use a 45-degree chamfering bit in the router table to soften the bottom inside and outside edges of the box. This routing will give the box a more finished look **(PHOTO A)**.

**2.** Cut the bottom panel to fit.

**ROUT A SMALL 45-DEGREE CHAMFER** on the inside and outside bottom edges of each piece. (This operation can also be done prior to making the miter cuts.)

**TAPE THREE CORNERS** of the box, spread glue on the miters, and roll them around the bottom panel into the finished form.

**USE RUBBER BANDS** to pull the corners tight until the glue sets. Leave the assembled boxes to dry for 45 minutes or more.

**3.** Sand all the inside surfaces that cannot be sanded after the box is assembled. These include the top and bottom sides of the Baltic birch bottom, the inside surfaces of all the box sides, and the chamfers on the inside edges of each part.

**4.** Tape the parts together flat on a work surface, spread glue on their miters and a bit in the grooves at each corner, and then roll the parts around the bottom into the form of the finished box **(PHOTO B )**.

**5.** Use rubber bands to hold the box together as the glue sets **(PHOTO C )**. Several layers of rubber bands can be used to build up clamping pressure.

# Make and fit a lift lid

**MAKE A LID FOR YOUR BOX FROM ¼-IN.-** thick figured wood. I selected spalted maple to contrast with the sycamore used for the body of this box.

**1.** Cut the lid to width using the tablesaw. You can use the materials list for this step or measure directly from the box. The profile of the lid should roll up directly from the profile at the top of the sides, so I determined the length and width of the lid on my box by measuring between the routed profiles on each side.

**2.** To cut the lid to length, use either the 90-degree crosscut sled on the tablesaw or the compound miter saw set at 90 degrees.

**3.** Use a ⅛-in. roundover bit in the router table to shape the top edges of the lid. Use a push block to keep the stock under control and your fingers a safe distance from the router bit. This is generally a safe operation because the bit is buried in the fence with very little of the cutting edge exposed. But the push block provides a margin of safety and greater control by keeping the stock from edging into the space between the bearing and the fence **(PHOTO A )**.

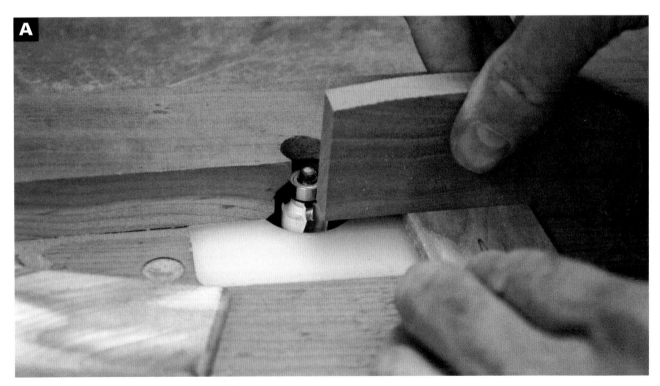

**ROUND THE TOP EDGES** of the box lid using the router table and a ⅛-in.-radius roundover bit.

FORM A RABBET on the edges of the lid to fit the top of the box. Raise the height of the cut until you get a perfect fit. Remember to rabbet the ends first.

DRILL THE HOLE in the lid for the tiny brass knob to fit.

**4.** Form a rabbet on the edge of the lid to fit the top of the box. The push block you made for the last operation will also work here to guide the lid along the tablesaw fence. Bury the blade slightly in a sacrificial fence clamped to the tablesaw fence. Then raise the blade to a sufficient height to make the cut (**PHOTO B**). For me, this is a trial-and-error operation. I set the blade just shy of the required height, make a test cut, and then raise the blade until I get a perfect fit. It's best to rabbet the ends of the lid first and then the sides so that any tearout caused by cutting the ends will be removed when the side rabbets are cut.

**5.** Mark the center of the lid and drill a ³⁄₁₆-in.-dia. hole ³⁄₁₆ in. deep for the brass pull, or make your own turned knob on the lathe from walnut or another contrasting hardwood (**PHOTO C**).

# The Same Bits, Two Distinct Boxes

You can also use other combinations of router bits to make stock for a tiny box. The boxes shown below were cut with a pair of router bits, using the same basic process as was used to make the lead box in this chapter. Combining a furniture-maker bit with a double roundover bit can provide an interesting molding shape. It is a simple design that can be used to make two boxes, each distinct from the other based on the way the molding is oriented in the box.

**1.** You will note that this molding has no flat surfaces on the outside **(PHOTO A )**, so cutting it to length on the tablesaw sled requires a different approach. First cut the various box parts to slightly longer than their finished length.

**2.** Because of the curved shape of this molding, both miter cuts are made inside face down with each end against the stop block **(PHOTO B )**. With the stop block in place, trim the miter at one end.

**TWO DIFFERENT ROUTER BITS** are used to create this molding. A furniture-maker bit at left and a double roundover bit at right.

**BOTH MITER CUTS** are made inside face down with each end against the stop block because of the curved shape of this molding.

USE A SHOPMADE HOLD-DOWN to control the stock while keeping your hands a safe distance away.

**3.** Turn the stock around to cut the other end. You can add a thin spacer between the stop block and workpiece during the second cut to make dead certain that the full miter is formed at each end. Use a spacer block between the stop block and workpiece when cutting the end pieces **(PHOTO C )**.

**4.** These boxes have no square surfaces on the outside where you can use clamps, so rubber bands are required to pull the corners tight while the glue sets. Check carefully that all the miters are closed (top and bottom) before you set the boxes aside for the glue to set. In some cases, clamps can be used over the rubber bands if additional clamping pressure is required **(PHOTO D )**.

RUBBER BANDS PULL the corners tight, but clamps come in handy in a pinch.

# A Routed Pen Box

Turning pens is a popular hobby among woodworkers. If you are a pen turner, you might enjoy making a fine box to hold one of your beautiful turned pens. In fact, with the right wood, careful shaping, and craftsmanship, the box can be as lovely as the pen itself. Even if you are not making the pen yourself, this box will hold a finely crafted collectible pen, perfect for the celebration of a special occasion, such as a graduation.

The maple box is routed to create a space for the pen to fit. This space is routed equally in both the body of the box and lid, using a core box bit and either a router table or plunge router with a guide with built in stops. In this chapter I'll demonstrate both techniques so that you may use either, based on the tools you have at hand. In both cases, stop blocks control the length of the cut, and the fence

(either on the router table or on the router itself) controls the exact position of the cut. The depth of the cut is established by the final height of the router bit either above the router table or at the deepest point of its cut. In woodworking there is always more than one way to accomplish any particular task, and I'll give you a few options with this box.

Using either method, it is best to reach the full depth of cut by

raising (or lowering) the router bit in steps, 1/8 in. at a time. The full depth necessary for most pens is less than 5/8 in., so routing in both the body of the box and the lid to an equal depth will only take three passes on the router table using a 3/4-in. core box bit. In addition to the maple box, I'll show you different ways this box can be designed to fit your own tastes. Choose your wood to accentuate the beauty of your pen.

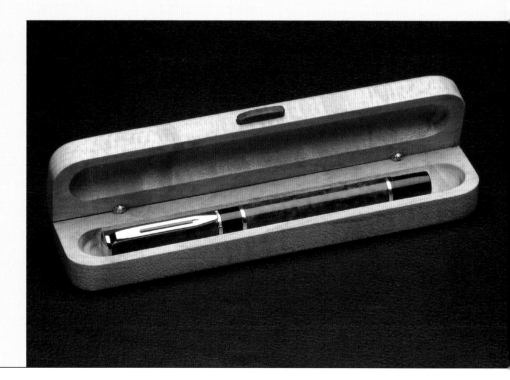

# Routed pen box

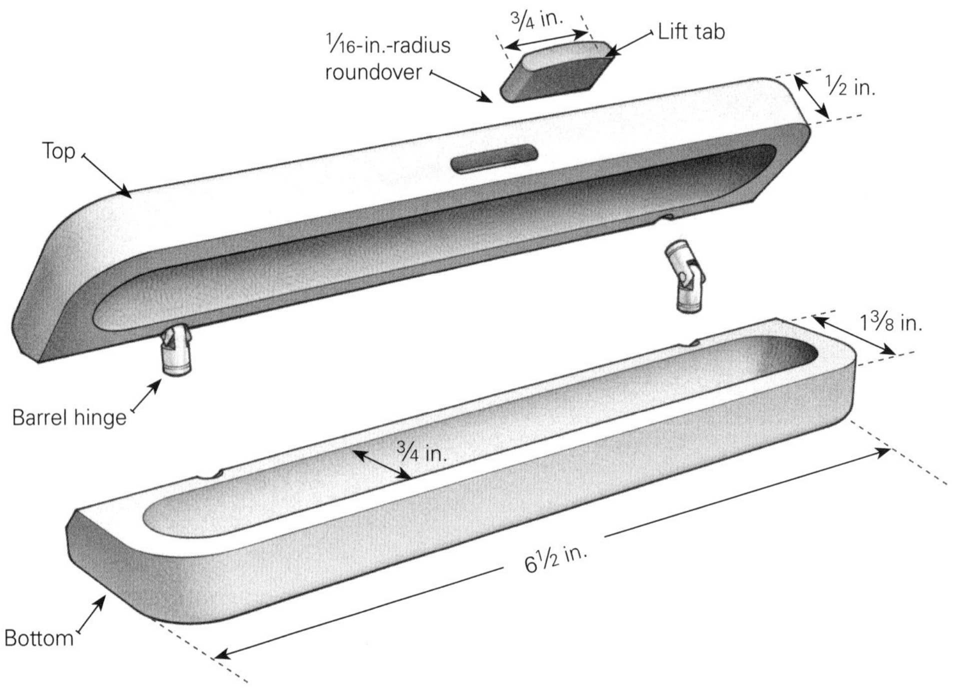

¾ in.
Lift tab
1⁄16-in.-radius roundover
½ in.
Top
1⅜ in.
Barrel hinge
¾ in.
6½ in.
Bottom


## MATERIALS

| QUANTITY | PART | MATERIAL | SIZE | NOTES |
|---|---|---|---|---|
| 1 each | Top and bottom | Maple or other hardwood | ½ in. x 1⅜ in. x 6½ in. | |
| 1 | Lift tab | Maple or other hardwood | ⅛ in. x ⅜ in. x ¾ in. | |
| 1 pair | 5mm barrel hinges | Brass | 5mm x 15mm | www.LeeValley.com, stock number 00D81.50 |

# Prepare the stock

**PREPARE YOUR STOCK BY PLANING IT TO**
½-in. thickness. Whether you plan to use the router table or plunge router to hollow the interior of the box will determine what comes next. Pay careful attention to the wood grain and color of wood as you select your parts, so they can be reassembled to appear as though your box has been cut from a single block of wood.

# Hollowing the inside on the router table

**1.** Cut the box parts to width and length. Use a crosscut sled on the tablesaw with a stop block to make certain that both the lid and bottom of the box are the same length **(PHOTO A )**. They must be exactly equal in length to successfully fit and install the 5mm mini barrel hinges later in the boxmaking process. You will also need to cut a story stick that will be used to set up the stop blocks on the drill press fence in a later step. For the story stick, cut one extra piece of wood to the same length as the top and bottom. This extra piece will not be routed for a pen to fit so it does not need to be exactly as thick or wide as the parts used to make the box.

**2.** Set up the router table with a ¾-in.-diameter core box bit and set the fence so that the opening from it to the center of the bit is 1 in. This setting will leave ¼ in. of material at the front of the box and slightly more at the back of the box where the hinges will fit. Proper setup for this operation is essential. Measuring from the center of the core box bit, the stops need to be equal distances on

**A** **USE A SLED AND STOP BLOCK** on the tablesaw to cut the parts for the pen box to equal lengths.

USE A ¾-IN.-DIAMETER core box bit to rout the inside of both the top and bottom of the box. Raise the bit in increments of ⅛ in. or less, while sliding the stock between stops.

THE FINISHED CUT should end ¼ in. from each end.

If I'm making a number of boxes at the same time, setting up stop blocks on the router table allows me to consistently rout multiple tops and bottoms with the same dimensions. This allows me to quickly and accurately make many versions of this same box.

both sides, and as it is rather difficult to find the exact center point of a core box bit, be prepared with a bit of scrapwood to make a test cut so you can adjust the stop blocks if necessary.

**3.** While holding the workpiece against the stop on the right—and using a push stick as shown to ensure it remains tightly against the fence—lower the piece into the cut (**PHOTO B**). Slide the piece along the fence to touch the stop block on the left, and then while still holding it tightly to the fence, turn the router off and let it stop before removing the piece.

**4.** It will take three passes each for both the lid and body of the box to achieve the full depth of ⅜ in. each. Between steps, raise the height of the router bit ⅛ in. The finished routing will provide full and equal depth to both parts (**PHOTO C**).

# Hollowing the inside with the plunge router

**USING THE PLUNGE ROUTER IS ALSO A** great way to make this box, and the advantage of this technique is that it's easier to watch what you are doing. Once the routing guide has been made, you can quickly make your box.

**1.** Plane the material to thickness and saw it to its finished width but not to its finished length. Then mark the locations for your box parts along the stock, leaving enough room between them to allow for them to be cut to final length. I leave about ¼ in. or more between parts. Mark the exact centerline of each box part. Before routing the parts, you will need to make a routing guide, as shown in the sidebar on p. 80.

**2.** Align the centerline of your box part with the exact centerline of the routing guide and clamp both the routing guide and the box stock to the workbench, being careful that the stock overhangs the edge of the workbench slightly so that the router fence follows the stock and not the bench **(PHOTO A )**. The fence is used to control the distance the routed groove is from the edge. The base plate of the router comes into contact with the two stops on the routing guide, which controls the length of the cut. Along with the centerline markings in the photo below you can also see the marks where the box parts will be cut from the strip to form the top and bottom of the box.

**AN ALTERNATE METHOD** for forming the inside space uses a plunge router and the same ¾-in.-diameter core box bit. The simple guide that provides stops is shown on p. 80. Mark the centerline of your box part on the stock and align it with the centerline on the guide.

The space between the blocks is determined as follows: Measure the router base diameter, add 6 in. for travel, and subtract the diameter of the router bit.

With my plunge router the width of the base is 6½ in. I add the 6 in. for travel. And I subtract ¾ in. for my router bit. This works out to 11¾ in. between stops.

## Routing guide

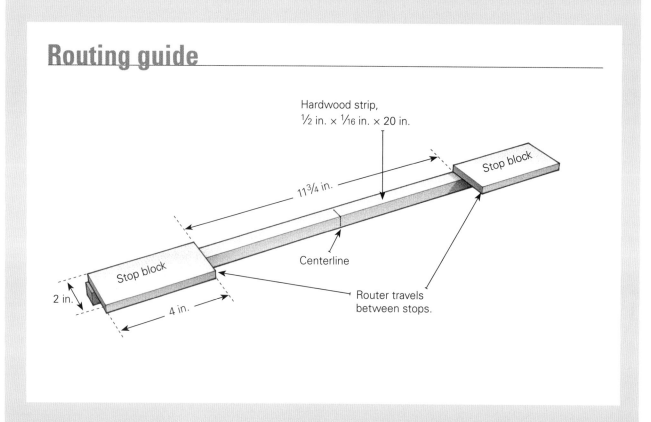

Hardwood strip,
½ in. × 1/16 in. × 20 in.

Stop block

11¾ in.

Stop block

Centerline

Router travels
between stops.

2 in.

4 in.

## MATERIALS

| QUANTITY | PART | MATERIAL | SIZE | NOTES |
|---|---|---|---|---|
| 1 | Hardwood strip | Hardwood | ½ in. x 1/16 in. x 20 in. | |
| 2 | Stop blocks | Hardwood | 3/8 in. x 2 in. x 4 in. | Glue in place. |

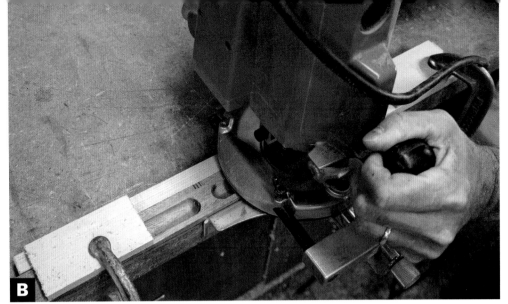

**PLUNGE THE ROUTER** into the cut in increments of no greater than ⅛ in. and to a full depth of ⅜ in.

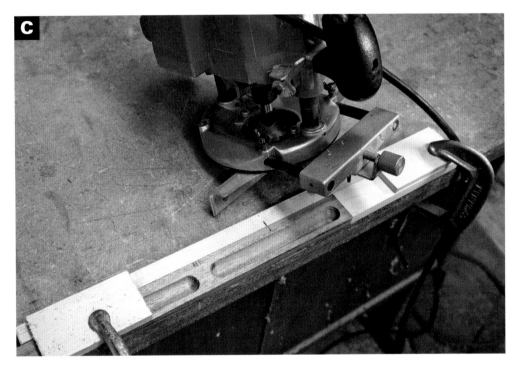

**MAKE CERTAIN THAT THE PEN BOX STOCK** extends beyond the fence. If it doesn't, a piece of stock of the same thickness and width can be used to provide smooth travel for the plunge router fence.

**3.** As in forming the inside of the box on the router table, plan to lower the core box bit into the cut in increments of no greater than ⅛ in., rather than trying to cut to the full depth of ⅜ in. all at once. Use a secure two-hand grip on the router, and move it toward you from left to right as you make each cut **(PHOTO B)**.

**4.** When you need to rout a piece near the end of the stock, a filler piece of the same dimensions can be used to provide smooth and secure travel for the router fence **(PHOTO C)**. Used either on the left or right as needed, the filler piece will prevent the router fence from dipping into an empty space and messing up the ends of the cut.

**5.** Cut the box parts to length using a stop block on the tablesaw sled so that each part will be exactly the same length. This is important. Then cut one extra piece of wood to the same length. This story stick will be used to set up the stop blocks on the drill press fence. This extra piece will not be routed for a pen to fit so it does not need to be exactly as thick or wide as the parts used to make the box.

# Drill for the hinges

**FOR THIS BOX I USED 5MM MINI BARREL** hinges. They are incredibly easy to use if you know the process of getting them perfectly aligned, but they can be a real challenge if you are relying on rulers or a tape measure to determine the location for the 5mm holes. If the holes are not perfectly aligned, the hinges can be tough to force into the holes and will not open and close as smoothly as you would like. To make them easy to install, I use a story stick technique using a piece of wood of the exact same length as the body and lid of the box. This technique allows for the exact placement of stop blocks along the fence of the drill press so that the hinges inserted in the body of the box will align perfectly with the holes drilled in the lid.

**1.** Set the position of the drill press fence. The fence location controls the distance of the hinges from the back of the box, and the strength of these hinges is due in part to them being surrounded by a sufficient amount of wood on all sides. For this box I set the tip of the 5mm brad point bit ³⁄₁₆ in. from the fence.

**2.** Next I set a stop block along the left side of the fence so that its distance from the tip of the drill bit is 5³⁄₄ in. Because the accuracy of this technique is based completely on the story stick, this dimension does not need to be exact.

**3.** While it is held firmly against the stop block at left, drill all the way through the story stick **(PHOTO A )**.

**4.** To locate the stop block on the other side, flip the story stick over, keeping the same edge against the fence. Lower the drill into the hole you drilled in step 3, and then hold the story stick firmly in place as you clamp the second stop block to the fence **(PHOTO B )**. Using the story stick in this manner, the stop block on the right will take its position from the first stop block on the left.

**USE A DRILL PRESS** to drill holes in the story stick for the 5mm mini barrel hinges. Drill all the way through the story stick stock while it is held against the stop block at left.

**FLIP THE STORY STICK** end over end and lower the drill bit into the hole just drilled. Then hold the story stick firmly in place without moving it as you add the stop block at right and clamp it firmly to the fence.

**C**

ONCE THE STOP BLOCKS ARE IN PLACE, left and right, adjust the depth of the drill. Some trial and error will be necessary to reach but not exceed a depth of half the full length of the hinge.

DRILL LEFT AND THEN RIGHT, sliding between the stop blocks, being careful to blow away any sawdust that might fall at the ends and interfere with the proper placement of the stock.

**D**

**5.** The 5mm mini barrel hinges require holes drilled to an exact depth on both parts, which is no deeper than one half the full length of the hinge. Using a dial caliper you will learn that they are $^{36}/_{64}$ in. long, so the holes should be drilled almost to a full depth of $^{9}/_{32}$ in. or $^{18}/_{64}$ in. deep. I give the dimension in 64ths because that is an easy dimension to read from a dial caliper. Adjust the depth of the hole using stock of the same thickness as the lid and bottom of the box. This may require several trial-and-error test drillings to get it just right, but you will find that the hinges work best when they are installed precisely to the correct depth **(PHOTO C)**.

**6.** Once the stop blocks have been set up using the story stick and the depth is set, you may proceed to drill both holes in the lid and both holes in the bottom of the box **(PHOTOS D & E)**. Move the stock from against one stop block

**E**

to the other in order to drill matching holes. Be very careful to clear away sawdust from drilling, as any that falls between the workpiece and either of the stop blocks can prevent the holes from being in the exact positions required. This operation should give you matching holes in both the lid and base, as shown below **(PHOTO F )**.

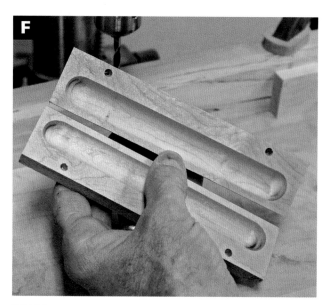

**WHEN PROPERLY DRILLED** for hinges, the top and bottom of the box will be perfect mirror images of each other.

**7.** Use a 45-degree chamfering router bit in the router table to make a chamfer at the back of the lid and bottom of the box to provide clearance for the hinges to operate **(PHOTO G )**.

**USE A 45-DEGREE CHAMFERING BIT** in the router table to rout the chamfer at the back of the box that allows the lid to open.

# Make a simple lift tab

**1.** I make a simple lift tab for opening the box by first routing a groove for it to fit into. Put a ⅛-in. straight-cut router bit in the router table and set the fence so that there is a ⅛-in. space between it and the router bit. Raise the router bit to a height of about ³⁄₁₆ in. above the router table. Then carefully measure to set stop blocks equidistant from both sides **(PHOTO A )**.

**2.** Hold the lid of the box tight to the fence and firmly against the stop block on the right. Lower the lid into the cut and move it from right to left to touch the stop block on the left. Then either slide the lid up and away from the bit, still holding it tight to the fence, or continue to hold it tight while you turn the router off and wait for it to stop **(PHOTOS B & C )**.

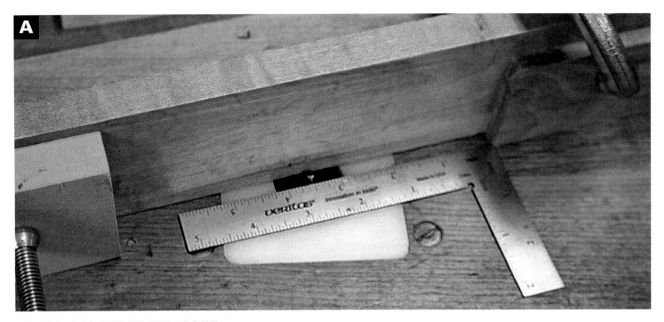

**ROUT A GROOVE AT THE FRONT** of the box for the lift tab. Measure carefully left and right so that the stop blocks are placed at an equal distance from the bit on each side.

**LOWER THE BOX LID** into the cut while holding it tightly against the fence. Move it from right to left through the cut and then lift it up from the bit, or turn the router off and wait for it to stop.

USE THE CUTOFF SLED on the tablesaw to cut tabs to length. Use a stop block to control the length of each cut. The eraser end of a pencil is used to control the loose part through the cut, and then is used to push the stock clear for the next cut.

USE A DISK SANDER to shape the lift tabs. The simple pivot device is screwed to a board clamped to the table of the disk sander. Use a pencil to hold the tab in the recess as you swivel the device against the sanding disk.

**3.** To make a simple lift tab for the lid, I use the sled on the tablesaw and thin stock cut to a thickness of ⅛ in., equal to the width of the router bit used to cut the recess for the tab to fit. Use a stop block to control the length of the cut and use the eraser end of a pencil to keep control of the tab throughout the cut (**PHOTO D**). I make these in a variety of woods so that I can choose either a matching or contrasting lift tab to go with any given box.

**4.** To gently round the face of the tab, use a swivel guide mounted to the table of a disk sander. To make this, cut a recess in the end of a piece of ¼-in. plywood and use a screw to secure it to a thicker piece of wood. The location of the screw attaching the upper piece to the lower determines the radius of the tab. Use a pencil and eraser to guide the tab through the operation while keeping your fingers a safe distance from the sanding disk (**PHOTO E**).

**5.** Use coarse sandpaper to begin rounding the edges so that the tab will fit exactly into the recess cut for it in the lid of the box. Use adhesive-backed sandpaper fastened to a flat surface (**PHOTO F**). I simply drag the end-grain corners over the coarse paper until they are rounded to the same shape as the recess. After I've achieved a close fit, I use finer sandpaper on a sanding block to remove the coarse marks from the heavy grit and to soften the edges of the front of the tab.

ROUND THE ENDS of the tab on coarse sandpaper and then use a finer grit with a sanding block to make it smooth and to soften the edges to the touch.

**6.** When you have a good fit, cut the tab to its finished length, using a tablesaw sled and stop block. I use a sharp awl to hold one end against the stop block and a thin piece of stock to hold down the other **(PHOTO G)**.

**7.** The finished tab can be glued into place after the final shaping and sanding of the box is complete. For now, test the fit but don't slide it all the way in. If you've gotten a close fit, it may not come out, and using pliers to pull it would mar the surface you worked so hard to sand **(PHOTO H)**.

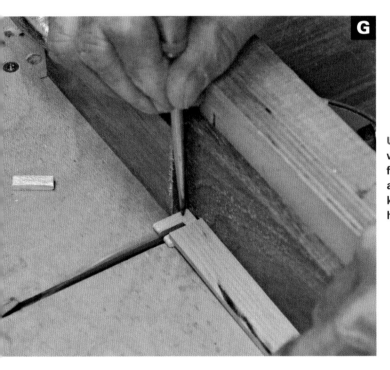

**USE THE SLED ON THE TABLESAW** with a stop block to cut the tab to its finished length. In this case, I use a sharp awl and an accessory hold-down block to keep the parts from flying around when hit by the saw.

**WHEN CUT TO LENGTH AND ROUNDED** on the ends to fit the mortise in the lid, the lift tab should be a perfect fit.

# Install the hinges

**1.** The installation of the hinges comes next. I use a squeeze bottle of glue to put a very small dab of glue in each hinge hole. This will lock the already tight-fitting hinges in place. Nurse the hinges into the holes on either the top or body of the box. Be careful that the hinges are oriented so that they bend at a 90-degree angle to the back of the box **(PHOTO A )**.

**2.** Use a hammer to tap the hinges down the rest of the way, being careful not to hit hard enough to make marks **(PHOTO B )**.

**3.** Next align the hinges in the holes on the opposite part of the box. Be careful that the hinges are going in straight before you apply any pressure. It can take some time to get the two hinges perfectly aligned in the holes, so be patient and you'll get the feel of it as they slide together. When they are nearly all the way in place, you can tap them closer using a mallet and wooden block to cushion the blow, or simply put the box in a vise and clamp tight, as shown below **(PHOTO C )**. No hinge could be lovelier in place **(PHOTO D )**.

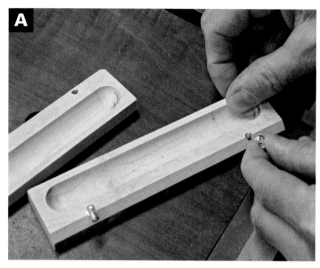

**PUT A SMALL DAB OF GLUE** in each hinge hole and then carefully position the hinges in place in the lid or bottom of the box.

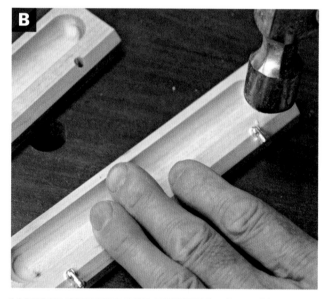

**LIGHTLY TAPPING THE HINGES** in place with a hammer is a good way to get them to seat to the full depth.

**CAREFULLY ALIGN THE HINGES** in the other part and begin to press gradually into place. To bring both parts into final position you may tap with a block of wood or squeeze the parts together in a vise, as shown here.

**ONE OF THE LOVELY THINGS** about this box is that the hinges, although effective, are so visually discrete, appearing as small spheres of brass.

# Shape the box

**AFTER THE BOX IS ASSEMBLED YOU CAN** begin shaping it on the router table. I use three different router bits for this operation.

**1.** Use a large ½-in.-radius roundover bit to rout the front corners of the box. Using a larger-diameter bit at the front corners gives the box a more pleasing shape. A backing board is required to square the box as it passes along the fence and to provide backing and prevent tearout during the cut **(PHOTO A )**. The top photo on p. 90 shows the full extent of routing with the larger bit **(PHOTO B )**.

**USE A ½-IN.-RADIUS ROUNDOVER BIT** in the router table to shape the front corners of the box. To stabilize the box on the router table and to prevent tearout, use a backing board.

**B**

**WITH THE CORNERS ROUNDED,** the box is ready for the next steps.

**C**

**USE A DISK SANDER** to smooth the ends and sand the front corners.

**2.** To clean up and even the edges from this routing operation, I use a disk sander. This also allows me to correct any slight misalignments that may have been introduced during the hinging operation **(PHOTO C )**.

**3.** I use two additional router bits in shaping this box. For the front edge and ends of the lid I rout with a ³⁄₁₆-in.-radius roundover bit **(PHOTO D )**. The ³⁄₁₆-in.-radius bit gives the front and ends of the box a smooth shape. For the back and bottom of the box I use a smaller-diameter ⅛-in.-radius bit. The difference may seem insignificant, but the larger profile at the front helps to draw attention to the front of the box. This, in association with the lift tab on the lid, helps the viewer to understand where the box should be opened and how it is to be viewed. I use the ⅛-in.-radius router bit on the back edge of the lid, the back corners, and all around the base of the box.

**D**

**I USE SMALLER ROUTER BITS** to shape the remaining edges of the box. The router bit used here has a $^3/_{16}$-in. radius.

# Sanding the box

**I USE A RANDOM-ORBITAL SANDER TURNED** upside down in a frame on the workbench to sand the box through 180-grit, 240-grit, and 320-grit sandpaper. I use the machine upside down because it is easier to hold a small box for sanding than to hold the sander. When the machine sanding is complete, soften the inside edges by lightly hand sanding with 320-grit sandpaper.

**SAND THE BOX** with a random-orbit sander. My own is held inverted in a frame on the workbench that allows for a vacuum to collect sanding dust.

# An Angular Version

You can make this box in a variety of woods, and choose either matching or contrasting lift tabs for a more dramatic effect. In addition, the outside shape of the box can be personalized to coordinate with the design of the pen you put in it. For example, a more angular box might be more appealing. To make this box with an angular shape I needed to allow for additional shaping at the front, so I used stock wider than that used in the standard pen box.

**1.** To make this box I used a cutting guide on the tablesaw to taper the box from the center toward the ends, thus achieving a different, more distinctive look. To make the cutting guide, use the pattern on the facing page to cut the shape out of a piece of ⅛-in. plywood on the bandsaw **(PHOTO A)**.

**2.** Cut the box top and bottom and rout out the inside as you would for the main box. For this box, however, the materials should be both longer and wider, as shown on the facing page.

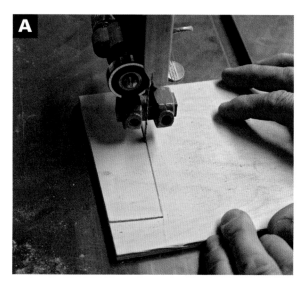

**USE THE BANDSAW** to cut a piece of ⅛-in. plywood to serve as a guide for holding the box on the sled as you cut the angled box to shape.

# An angular routed pen box

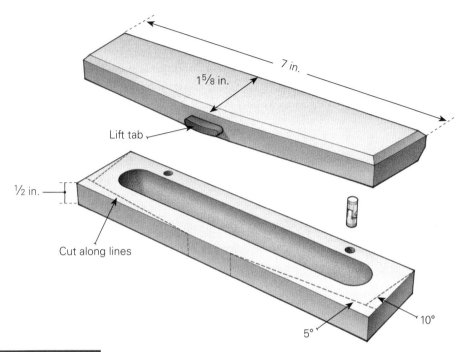

7 in.

1⁵/₈ in.

Lift tab

½ in.

Cut along lines

5°

10°

## MATERIALS

| QUANTITY | PART | MATERIAL | SIZE | NOTES |
|---|---|---|---|---|
| 1 each | Top and bottom | Sycamore | ½ in. x 1⁵/₈ in. x 7 in. | |
| 1 | Lift tab | Maple or other hardwood | ⅛ in. x ⅜ in. x ¾ in. | |
| 1 pair | 5mm barrel hinges | Brass | 5mm x 15mm | www.LeeValley.com, stock number 00D81.50 |

# Cutting guide for angled pen box

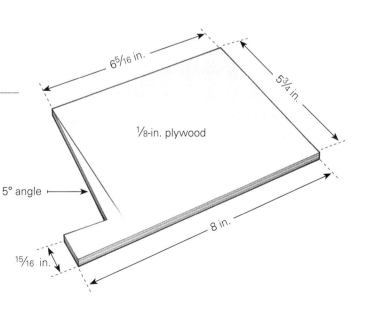

6⁵/₁₆ in.

5¾ in.

⅛-in. plywood

5° angle

8 in.

¹⁵/₁₆ in.

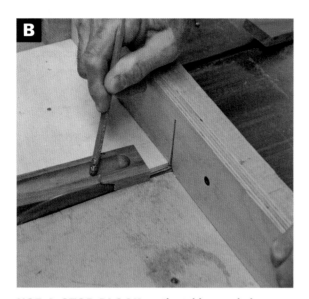

USE A STOP BLOCK on the tablesaw sled to position the plywood cutting guide so that the front edge of the box is held in the correct position as you make your cuts.

**3.** Rout the small recess for the lift tab to fit the box lid. This should be done before the next step.

**4.** Set the stop block on the tablesaw sled to position the cutting guide. Use a pencil to hold the lid so that it is nested in the guide as you make the required cuts, and then do the same for the bottom of the box. Each part must be cut twice, first along the front at one end and then the other to form the shape **(PHOTO B )**. When cut, the lid and bottom of the box will be mirror images of each other **(PHOTO C )**.

**5.** Use the miter gauge on the tablesaw to angle the ends of the box parts **(PHOTO D )**.

EACH PART OF THE BOX requires two cuts.

**6.** Before sanding and finishing, use a chamfering router bit to complete the angled effect **(PHOTO E )**. As in making the main box in this chapter, I vary the size of the chamfer, making a larger cut on the front and ends and a lighter cut at the back and along the bottom edge.

**USE THE MITER GAUGE** on the tablesaw to trim the ends of the box top and bottom to shape.

**IN KEEPING WITH THE ANGULAR SHAPE** of this box, I used a 45-degree chamfering bit in the router table to shape the edges, making a heavier cut along the front and ends and a lighter cut on the rest of the edges.

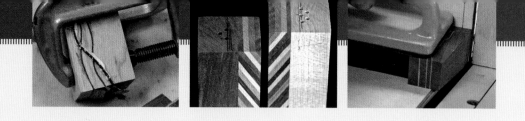

# Salt and Pepper Shakers

One of the easiest ways to form a hollow space for the interior of a box is to use a Forstner bit in a drill press or lathe. We'll be using this technique to create a set of salt and pepper shakers, but this technique can be used to make boxes in general for a variety of uses. A Forstner bit is designed to drill a nearly flat-bottomed hole, and the bits come in rather large sizes. For instance, this salt and pepper set was hollowed using a ⅞-in. Forstner bit and drilled to a depth of 2¹⁄₁₆ in. using a drill press.

The most challenging task with this kind of box is fitting the lid. Drilling a hole is easy; filling it with a tight-fitting lid is more complex. You can turn lids on the lathe, which takes some practice and a great deal of exacting attention. But I've made fitting the lid of this box much easier by using a routing guide for the router table. The easy-to-make guide adjusts to create lids to an exact fit perfectly again and again and without the trial and error that comes with fitting lids on the lathe.

For this project, I use bandsaw cuts and veneers to form intersecting patterns in the wood, and the same techniques can be used to make boxes for other purposes. Years ago I was asked by a friend to make a box to hold two or three tablespoons of her father's remains to carry a bit of his ashes to release in the Ganges River. I made a simple turned box on the lathe similar to the one shown in the Design Options at the end of this chapter. Again, the key to making this box is the Forstner bit used to hollow the inside, and the simple routing guide used to form the perfectly fitting lid.

# Salt and pepper shakers

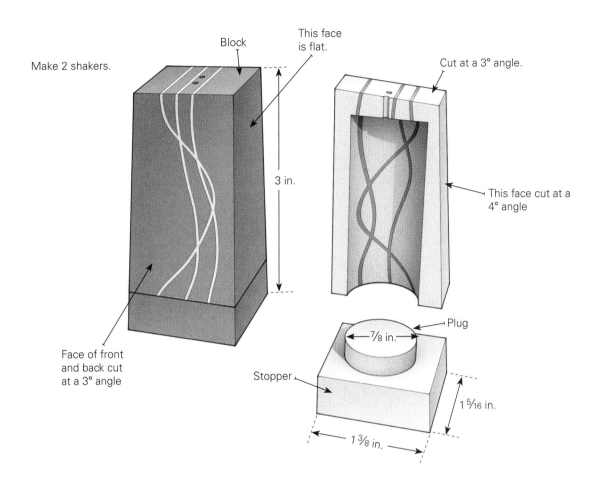

Make 2 shakers.

Block

This face is flat.

3 in.

Face of front and back cut at a 3° angle

Cut at a 3° angle.

This face cut at a 4° angle

Plug

⁷/₈ in.

Stopper

1 ⁵/₁₆ in.

1 ³/₈ in.

## MATERIALS

| QUANTITY | PART | MATERIAL | SIZE | NOTES |
|---|---|---|---|---|
| 1 | Block | Walnut | 1½ in. × 1½ in. × 2⅝ in. | |
| 1 | Block | Maple | 1½ in. × 1½ in. × 2⅝ in. | |
| 1 | Stopper | Walnut | 1¾ in. × 1¾ in. × ⅝ in. | Will be cut to final size in a later step |
| 1 | Stopper | Maple | 1¾ in. × 1¾ in. × ⅝ in. | Will be cut to final size in a later step |
| 6 pieces | Maple and walnut veneers* | | 1½ in. × 3½ in.** | |

*Or other contrasting colors.
**Grain should run in the short direction.

# Decorate the stock with embedded veneers

**USE A BANDSAW** with a ¼-in. blade to make meandering cuts through the pieces of walnut and maple stock.

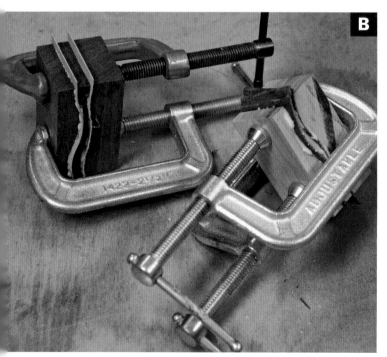

**GLUE PIECES OF CONTRASTING VENEER** into the cuts and clamp tightly until the glue dries. In order for the veneers to make the required bend, the grain must be oriented at a 90-degree angle to the direction of the grain in the blocks.

**1.** Begin with equal-size blocks of maple and walnut, and cut each into three pieces using a bandsaw with a ¼-in. blade to make meandering cuts that will be filled with contrasting veneer. The bandsaw kerf and the thickness of the veneer will be close enough to the same width that the veneer will fill the kerf when the blocks are glued back together. It is important in this process that the curves be smooth and gradual, and that the first two cuts do not cross. If they do, you will have difficulty gluing the pieces back together **(PHOTO A)**.

**2.** Use dark wood veneer for the maple block and light wood for the walnut block. Cut the pieces of veneer wide enough and long enough to fill the cut to its full length and width. In order for this process to work, the veneer's grain must be at a 90-degree angle to the grain of the blocks, as the veneer's grain will not bend easily enough in the other direction to follow the curves.

**3.** Spread glue on each of the cut surfaces of the blocks and sandwich a layer of contrasting veneer between each block layer. While gluing, make sure that all the edges of the original blocks align **(PHOTO B)**.

**4.** When the glue has dried, sand the blocks flush and then make a fresh bandsaw cut through each block, using the same sort of smooth curve. Cut through the previous veneered lines to create an interesting finished design. Glue in another layer of veneer and clamp tightly with the edges aligned **(PHOTO C)**.

**5.** After the glue has dried and the clamps have been removed, sand the blocks and make sure they are square and equal in size **(PHOTO D)**.

MAKE AN ADDITIONAL BANDSAW CUT through each block, crossing back and forth over the previous cuts. Then glue the contrasting veneers in place.

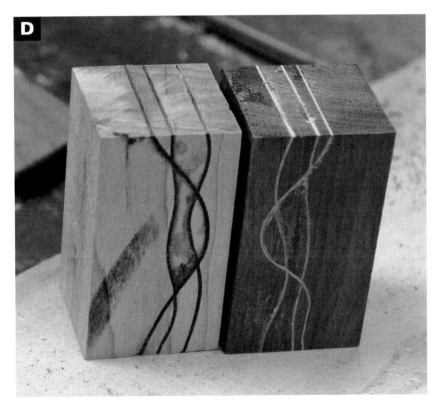

SAND THE MAPLE AND WALNUT BLOCKS smooth to prepare them for the next step. The ends must be square to the sides.

# Drill holes to form the interiors

**USE A ⅞-IN. FORSTNER BIT IN THE DRILL** press to drill to a depth just ¼ in. shy of the full length of the block. The remaining ¼ in. will be where the holes are drilled for the salt and pepper to come out. It will also allow for some shaping to be done at the top of each box. I use a fence and stop block to position the blocks on the drill press. Because the finished profile of the shakers is rectangular rather than square, I mark to drill an equal distance from three sides.

**USE A FENCE AND STOP BLOCK** on the drill press to position the hole near the center of the stock.

# Make the stoppers

**I MAKE THE STOPPERS FROM MAPLE AND** walnut stock with the grain running parallel to the blocks that form the upper portions of the shakers. The stopper stock must be slightly larger in both thickness and width than the blocks used to make the body of each shaker. This allows for the stopper to be trimmed or sanded to size after the plug is formed to fit the interior.

**1.** Use the sled on the tablesaw to cut the walnut and maple stoppers. The stop block clamped to the sled controls the length of the cut. I use the eraser end of a pencil to hold the small stock safely against the stop block while keeping my fingers a safe distance from the blade **(PHOTO A)**.

**2.** To locate the center of each stopper for drilling, use a pencil and straight edge to mark from corner to corner.

**USE THE SLED** on the tablesaw with a stop block to cut the stock for the stopper.

**3.** To begin fitting the stoppers, drill a small pilot hole at the center you just marked in each stopper, being careful to set the drill so it does not go all the way through. I use a number 4 finish nail with the head clipped off as the drill bit, as a similarly clipped nail will be used in a later step as the pivot pin in the shop-made routing guide used to fit the stopper to the hole bored in the body of each box **(PHOTO B )**.

**4.** Clamp the workpiece in place on the router guide (see the sidebar on p. 102) so it can be rotated into the spinning router bit. I use a ¾-in. straight-cut router bit with a bearing of equal size on the shaft. This bearing keeps the router bit from cutting beyond the intended range of the guide **(PHOTO C )**.

**5.** Turn the workpiece in a counter-clockwise direction and pivot the guide very slowly into the cut so that the stock is removed in a gradual manner. The stop block shown in the bottom left photo **(PHOTO D )** is used to control the diameter of the plug formed on the stock. It may take one or more practice setups to get exactly the right fit. Move the stop block forward to increase the diameter of the plug and tighten the fit, or move the stop block away very slightly to make the plug smaller and get a looser fit. By using this guide you can achieve the level of tightness you prefer. The finished stock will look like that shown in the bottom right photo **(PHOTO E )**.

**MARK LINES FROM ONE CORNER** to the other on the maple and walnut blocks to locate where to drill guide holes, then drill the guide holes with the drill press.

**THE STOCK WILL TURN** on the guide pin as you very slowly pivot the fence into the router bit.

**USE A TOGGLE CLAMP** to hold the lid stock down on the guide pin, and turn the stock in a counter-clockwise direction.

**THE GUIDE PIN POSITIONS** the stock and the stop block is used to control the diameter. Move it forward to tighten the fit and back to make the lid fit more loosely.

## Lid-shaping guide

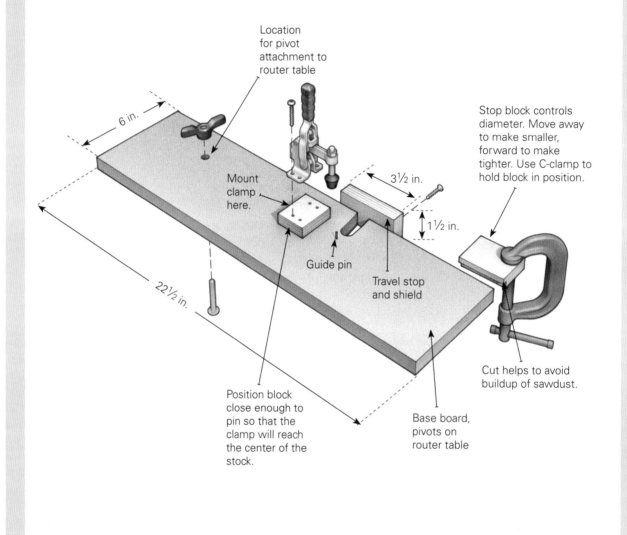

Location for pivot attachment to router table

6 in.

Mount clamp here.

Guide pin

22½ in.

Position block close enough to pin so that the clamp will reach the center of the stock.

Stop block controls diameter. Move away to make smaller, forward to make tighter. Use C-clamp to hold block in position.

3½ in.

1½ in.

Travel stop and shield

Base board, pivots on router table

Cut helps to avoid buildup of sawdust.

It can be challenging to get just the right fit on a lid or on a plug for the bottom of a salt and pepper shaker. They can be turned on the lathe with some skill and patience, but this guide for the top of a router table will give more reliable results and allow you to fine-tune an exact fit. Cut your parts as shown in the drawing. For those who have a more standard router table than my own, this technique requires you to drill a pivot hole in the top for a pivot point attachment of the guide to the router table.

You will need a ¾-in. straight-cut router bit with a bearing on the shaft equal to the diameter of the router bit.

**1.** Mount the base board to the router table using a ⅜-in. carriage bolt and knob. If your router table is not equipped with a pivot fence, please refer to the sidebar on p. 65, as it is easy to add to most router tables. Leave it loose enough that it will move as you pivot it into the cutter.

**2.** With the router bit raised only slightly above the router table, rout into the base board only about 2 in. and then stop. Use a stop block to control the amount of movement or rotation as you are preparing for the first use.

**3.** Gradually raise the router bit in increments, each time rotating the base board into the cut until the router bit reaches the full thickness of the base board. Then use screws to install the piece identified in the drawing as the travel stop and shield. This piece keeps your fingers from touching the spinning router bit and also keeps the movement of the pivot board within a controlled range.

**4.** Carefully measure for the placement of the guide pin. The distance between the guide pin and the router bit should equal the radius of the intended lid or plug. For the salt and pepper shakers, requiring holes drilled ⅞ in. diameter, the correct radius would be ⁷⁄₁₆ in., but I prefer to put the pin slightly closer so that the exact diameter of the plug is controlled by the use of a stop block. The stop block allows the user to fine-tune the exact fit. Use a C-clamp to secure the stop block in place, as other clamps may allow the block to move slightly during this operation.

**5.** In use, the stock should be rotated in a counterclockwise direction to maintain complete control. The router should be started while the bearing is against the travel stop, and the rotation should begin as you move the workpiece into range of the cutter. Work in slow increments, turning the stock a full rotation and then easing the guide slightly closer to the stop block as you begin the next rotation. Keep your fingers safely on the operator side of the guide.

WORK SMART

To locate the center of a piece, as you need to do with the stoppers, use a pencil and straightedge to draw a diagonal line from one corner to the other. Then draw another diagonal line crossing from corner to corner in the other direction. Where these lines meet in the middle is your center.

# Trim the stoppers and shape the boxes

FIT THE STOPPER in the salt and pepper boxes and use the bandsaw to trim the edges even with the sides. Some additional sanding will be needed.

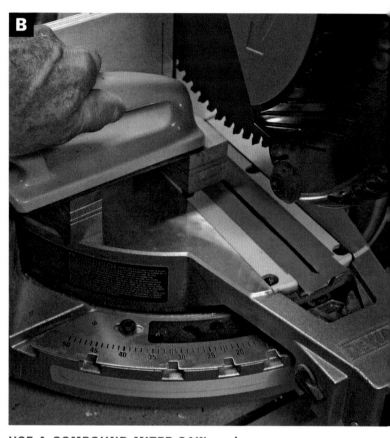

USE A COMPOUND MITER SAW, as shown, or a tablesaw miter gauge to trim the front and back of the box at a 3-degree angle. Use a hold-down block to hold the boxes in position and to keep your hands a safe distance from the blade.

**1.** Fit each stopper in its box and use the bandsaw to trim the stoppers to roughly conform to the dimensions of the box. I keep the cutline far enough from the edges of the block so that the parts can be sanded flush on the belt and disk sanders (**PHOTO A**).

**2.** Shaping the boxes can be done either using a miter gauge on the tablesaw or using a compound miter saw (**PHOTO B**). See the sidebar on p. 19 for instructions on how to perform this task safely. Note the zero-clearance fence used on the compound miter saw, which provides a clear point of alignment. Using a hold-down block to keep my

A zero-clearance fence is used with the compound miter saw to give full support to the stock being cut to shape.

C

**TO MAKE THE FINAL TRIMMING CUTS,** support the ends of the boxes with a ⅛-in.-thick strip of wood. Adjust the position of the strip to hold the bases tightly against the fence.

hands a safe distance from the blade, I trim the front and back of each block at a 3-degree angle so that each tapers toward the top.

**3.** I taper the outer side of each shaker so that they will look like a set when they are nested together. Taper the side offset so that the shakers narrow toward the top. Trim the block to conform to the drawing on p. 97. To make this cut accurately requires the blocks to be supported at the top with a ⅛-in.-thick strip of wood, so that the base will be held tightly to the fence on the compound miter saw. I set the angle of the cut at 4 degrees and then make an additional angle cut across the top, at about 3 degrees. Note in the photo above **(PHOTO C)** that the edge of the base is aligned with the zero-clearance fence so that the correct amount of material will be removed to give the salt and pepper shakers their interesting shape.

# Drill holes for the salt and pepper

**USE THE DRILL PRESS AND A ¹⁄₁₆-IN. BIT TO** drill the holes in the top for the salt and pepper. For food safety, and to keep the taste of finishes from affecting the taste of the salt or pepper, clear shellac should be used to finish the inside and outside of each box after sanding.

**DRILL HOLES** for the salt and pepper to pass through.

## DESIGN OPTIONS

## Multicolored salt and pepper shakers

**1.** Either use material left over from making the inlay on p. 17 or follow the technique in that chapter to create two matching blocks of multi-colored wood. To build the patterned block necessary for this project will require about 20 strips of wood ⅛ in. thick and 1½ in. wide.

**2.** Cut smaller blocks about ½ in. thick from the larger multicolored block already prepared. Use the miter gauge on the tablesaw set at 50 degrees. Use a block clamped to the fence as your guide piece so that when the stock passes through the saw it is not trapped between the blade and the fence, which would lead to the serious risk of kickback (**PHOTO A**). After making the cut, stop the saw before removing the piece.

**3.** Glue the multicolored stock to blocks of solid wood. Your success in this technique is not dependent on making your shakers a particular size or shape. I used solid wood blocks of walnut

**CUT A PIECE FROM THE INLAY STOCK** featured in the Hinged Pocket Box chapter to begin making a multicolored salt and pepper set. The block of wood clamped to the tablesaw fence allows the stock to be positioned on the miter gauge and then prevents the loose cutoff piece from being trapped between the blade and fence.

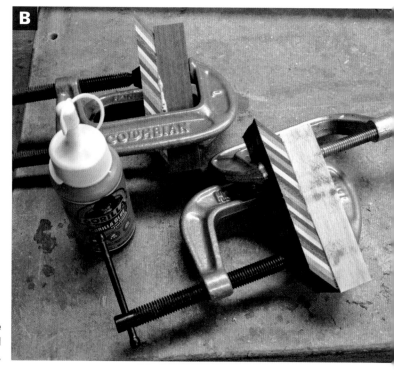

**GLUE AND CLAMP** the multicolored pieces to walnut and maple stock to begin forming blocks.

and maple to begin forming the two parts of the set and chose to make mine ⅞ in. thick and 1½ in. wide **(PHOTO B )**.

**4.** Use the tablesaw to square the edges of the pattern block to conform to the width of the walnut and maple blocks, and trim the glued-up blocks to size so that they are rectangular in shape. Use a push block to safely guide the stock through the cut **(PHOTO C )**.

**5.** Use the sled on the tablesaw to cut the blocks to length. First square one end and then use a stop block to control the length of the next cuts so that both shakers will be exactly the same size **(PHOTO D )**.

**6.** Use the drill press and Forstner bit to drill a flat-bottomed hole into the endgrain of each piece. The depth should be set to leave only about ³⁄₁₆ in. to ¼ in. of stock **(PHOTO E )**.

**7.** Follow the directions in the main project to make the plugs for the ends.

**8.** After fitting the stoppers drill the holes for the salt and pepper to come out.

**AFTER GLUING** the multicolored stock to pieces of solid wood, trim the edges to align on the tablesaw.

**USE EITHER THE COMPOUND MITER SAW** or the tablesaw with sled and stop block to trim the blocks to length.

**TO FINISH THE SET,** drill the interior space.

# A turned memory box

You can make beautiful turned boxes using similar drilling techniques while turning the shape on the lathe. Because this box won't be a shaker, I used the end plug on top and didn't drill any salt and pepper holes. Despite the fact that I'm making this tiny box to hold crematory remains, it is particularly fun to make. Please see the next chapter for additional information on lathe-turned boxes.

**1.** Use a 1-in. Forstner bit in the chuck on the lathe to drill a hole in the stock **(PHOTO A )**.

**2.** Make a stopper with a plug on one end using the router technique shown on p. 100. Put the lid in place and shape the exterior of the box, including the shape of the lid, between lathe centers **(PHOTO B )**.

**3.** When you have achieved a pleasing shape, sand your box smooth **(PHOTO C )**.

**4.** Polish and wax the box while it is still on the lathe **(PHOTO D )**.

**5.** I added a decorative pull to the top of my box. Use the technique shown on p. 120 to drill a hole in the lid of the turned box to form a mortise so that the small pull can be added.

**USE A FORSTNER BIT in the lathe to drill the interior space for a turned box.**

**FORM A STOPPER PIECE** for the lid in the same way you made the bottom for the salt and pepper shakers, and put it in place between lathe centers as you shape the body of the box.

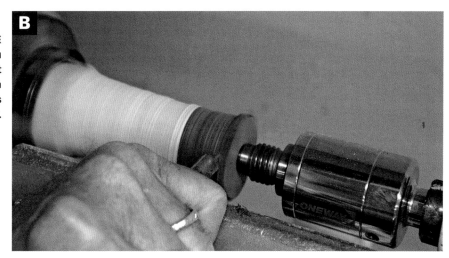

**WHEN YOU HAVE FORMED** a shape that you like, use a strip of coarse sandpaper to begin sanding.

**WORK YOUR WAY THROUGH** a progression of grits until you reach a final polish using wax.

**TO TURN A SMALL FINIAL** in the shape of a cross, begin with this shape. The final shape comes with a bit of sanding.

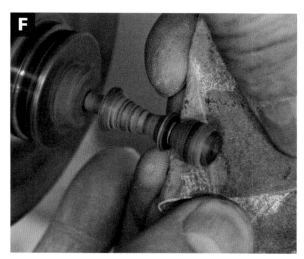

**TO FORM A HEART-SHAPED FINIAL,** begin by making an apple shape with a dimple in the end-grain.

**AFTER SANDING THE SURFACE** of the apple flat, the heart shape appears.

**SAW THE CROSS** off the stock so that it can be mounted in the lid of the box. Mount either the cross or the heart shape to the top of your box.

**6.** To turn a cross for the top of the crematory box, turn a shape as shown in the top left photo above **(PHOTO E )**. I use a set of lathe tools intended for turning pens, as these provide a more delicate touch. A very small gouge and skew chisel are useful for such fine work. When the pull is complete with tenon and removed from the lathe, simply sand it on both sides. The disk turned on the shaft will form a cross shape when flattened on both sides. To turn a heart-shaped finial, begin by turning a

small apple shape on the end of your turning stock **(PHOTO F )**. When you sand one surface flat, as shown in the bottom left photo above, a heart shape is revealed **(PHOTO G )**.

**7.** After turning and sanding on both sides, use a saw to cut the cross or heart loose from the turning stock **(PHOTO H )**. Mount your cross or heart on the top of your box.

# A Satellite Ring Box

Years ago I turned a box like this one and put a sapphire ring inside for my wife. I'm not sure where the ring is kept when it's not being worn, but I do know that the box found a special place where it is kept on display. I call it a satellite ring box because it vaguely resembles something that might have been launched into space. It's turned on the lathe and is both fun and challenging to make. As with most lathe work, some practice may be required to hone your skills before you begin. But practice is all part of the fun and the results will be gratifying.

Besides a lathe, you will need a few common lathe tools: a faceplate, a drill chuck, and a chuck with spigot jaws. I like to use tight-grained beautiful woods for turning these boxes, and small scraps from larger projects are worth saving for projects just like this.

# Satellite ring box

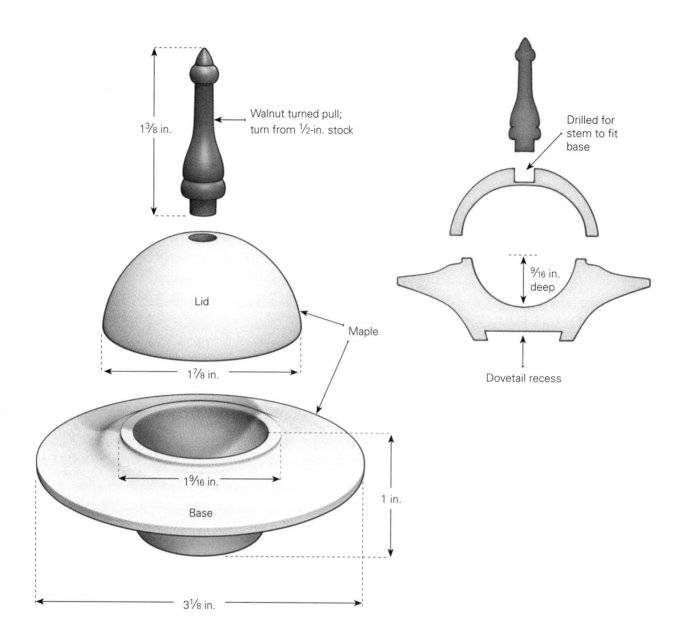

1³⁄₈ in.

Walnut turned pull;
turn from ¹⁄₂-in. stock

Lid

1⁷⁄₈ in.

Maple

1⁹⁄₁₆ in.

Base

1 in.

3¹⁄₈ in.

Drilled for
stem to fit
base

⁹⁄₁₆ in.
deep

Dovetail recess

## MATERIALS

| QUANTITY | PART | MATERIAL | SIZE | NOTES |
| --- | --- | --- | --- | --- |
| 1 | Base | Maple | 1 in. × 3½ in. × 3½ in. | Start with a slightly larger block. Cut to final size in a later step. |
| 1 | Lid | Maple | 1 in. × 2¼ in. × 2¼ in. | Start with a slightly larger block. Cut to final size in a later step. |
| 1 | Turned pull | Walnut | ½ in. × ½ in. × 2 in. | Necessary starting size |

# Prepare the stock

**1.** Begin by cutting your stock. I cut a block only slightly larger than the size of the base in the materials list, and then cut a smaller block to make the lid. Cutting your stock only slightly larger than is required speeds the process and reduces waste.

**2.** Find the center of both your lid and base stock. To do so, draw diagonal lines from each corner to the other. Where these two lines intersect will be the center of the stock **(PHOTO A)**.

**3.** Use a drill press and a ¼-in. drill bit to drill holes at the centers of both pieces about ¼ in. deep. This is to accommodate the short dowel that will be used to center the stock on the faceplate **(PHOTO B)**.

**4.** With a compass centered on the hole at the center of the stock, mark a circle to the edge of each piece **(PHOTO C)**. This line will guide your bandsaw cut as you rough out the stock.

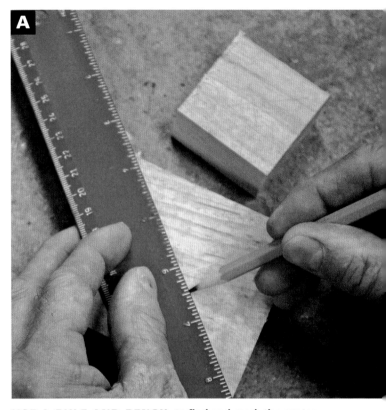

**USE A RULE AND PENCIL** to find and mark the center of the stock. If you draw a line from one corner to the other, and then across from corner to corner in the other direction, where they cross will be dead center.

**USE A ¼-IN. DRILL** to make a hole in the center, about ¼ in. deep.

**USE A COMPASS** to mark a circle. I set the width of the compass to align with the edge of the stock.

USE THE BANDSAW to cut away the corners of the turning stock.

USE DOUBLE-FACED CARPET TAPE to adhere the turning stock to a block mounted on the faceplate.

**5.** Cut the turning blanks into circles on the bandsaw. This will speed the turning operation and help to avoid a catch that would loosen the grip of the faceplate on the stock (**PHOTO D**).

**6.** Use double-faced carpet tape to secure the turning stock, starting with the stock for the base, to the block of wood screwed to the faceplate (see the sidebar on the facing page). I cut a hole in the center of the tape to provide clearance for the dowel mounted in the block of wood (**PHOTO E**).

**7.** Align the turning stock so that it fits the dowel at the center of the faceplate and press it in place (**PHOTO F**). The small dowel in the center of the faceplate provides a point of alignment but also prevents lateral motion from the pressure applied by the tool. This technique relies on both the double-faced tape and the tail center to hold the material safely in place, and is effective for making a tiny box. It would not be safe if using much larger materials.

NOTE THE DOWEL MOUNTED in the center of the block. This will hold the turning stock in alignment at the center.

A shopmade wooden faceplate with a dowel at the center is a useful tool to hold small flat parts on the lathe, when used with double-faced carpet tape. The dowel at the center keeps the part from shifting as pressure from the gouge is applied, and the double-faced tape holds the part secure to the faceplate. One major advantage of this setup is that the part can be pried loose without damage when the step is complete.

To make a wooden faceplate for turning the base and lid of this box, simply screw a block of wood to the steel or iron faceplate that came with your lathe. Turn it to a round shape and then use the drill chuck mounted in the tailstock to drill a ¼-in. hole at the center. Insert a ¼-in. dowel in the center so that it protrudes about ³⁄₁₆ in. to ¼ in. Glue the dowel in place for a secure fit. This operation resembles the technique used to

drill into the lid for the pull. Drill a dowel hole at the center of the workpiece. Then, to secure the workpiece to the faceplate, simply cut a hole in the center of a piece of double-faced tape and stick it to the faceplate. Press the workpiece in place. Use a C-clamp to apply clamping pressure so that the tape gets a good grip. To remove the workpiece, simply pry it loose.

## Wooden faceplate

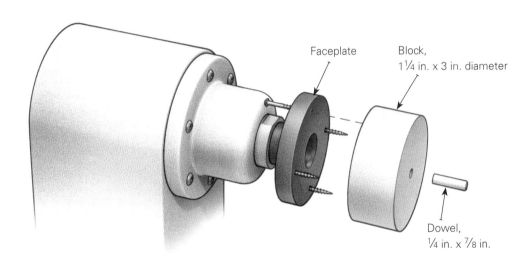

Faceplate

Block,
1¼ in. x 3 in. diameter

Dowel,
¼ in. x ⅞ in.

# Shape the bottom of the box

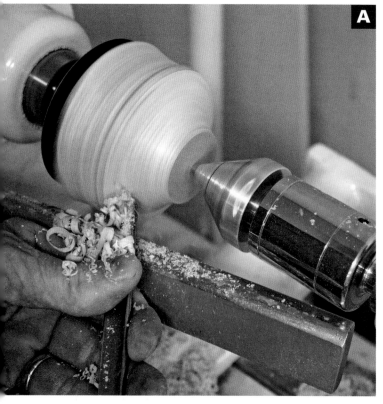

**USE THE LIVE CENTER** on the tailstock to hold the turning piece tightly to the faceplate as you begin defining the shape of the satellite box.

**1.** Begin by shaping the base of the box. I use a spindle gouge for this, with the stock held securely between the faceplate on one end and the live center at the other. The tail center keeps the body of the box from coming loose from the tape during the most aggressive part of the operation (**PHOTO A**). The tool rest should be placed as closely as possible for better control, but check the rotation before turning on the lathe to make sure the stock does not touch. I am aiming to create smooth curves as I begin defining the shape of the base.

**2.** After the bulk of the tool work is completed on the underside of the base, sand it, working from coarse to medium through fine grits. Then move the tail center away and use a small skew chisel to cut a recess at the bottom of the box sized to fit the spigot jaws on the chuck (**PHOTO B**). The recess for the spigot chuck should be slightly tapered toward the inside and flat on the bottom so that the jaws will grip tightly. Despite removing the tail center from the stock, a light touch with the chisel and steady pressure against the double-faced tape will keep the stock on the faceplate.

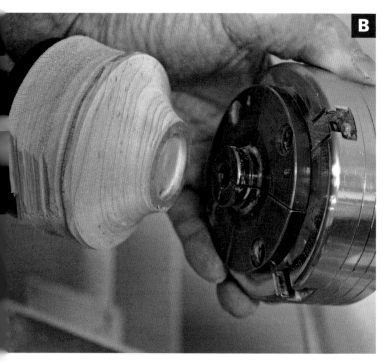

**SHAPE THE BOTTOM** of the satellite ring box to fit the spigot jaws. The hole at the underside should be deep enough for the chuck to get a good grip and slightly angled (wider toward the inside) so that the dovetail-shaped jaws will hold tightly.

Be sure to wear a full face shield when turning wood on the lathe. If a piece came loose, it could be dangerous.

# Hollow the inside of the box

**1.** Clamp the base to the lathe using the spigot chuck. I use a gouge to hollow the inside of the box. Cut the hollow about 1⅛ in. to 1¼ in. in diameter and about 9/16 in. deep. Do this carefully, as an aggressive cut will cause a catch and break the box loose from the spigot jaws (**PHOTO A**).

**2.** The lid will overlap a small raised area on the top of the base; shape the top side of the base with this in mind. To finish where the lid will rest, use a small skew chisel to shape a small tongue and a flat spot for the lid (**PHOTO B**).

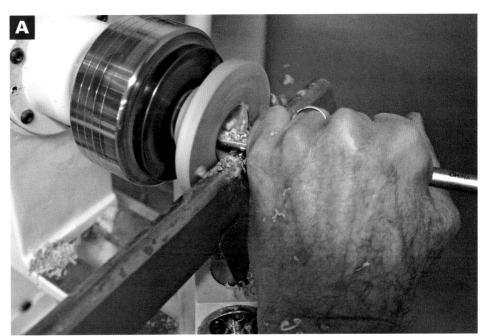

**USE A GOUGE** to form the recess for what will become the inside of the box.

**SHAPE THE TOP SIDE** of the body of the box and then use a skew chisel to form the raised lip where the lid will fit.

# Turn the lid

**TO MAKE THE LID, FIRST GIVE IT A ROUGH** shape and then form a spigot on the top so that the spigot jaws can get a good grip for the next step.

**1.** Remove the base from the faceplate and put the lid on in the same manner, using fresh double-faced carpet tape to provide a good grip. The hole drilled on the underside of the lid stock fits the pin centered in the faceplate block. Rough out the basic lid shape with a gouge.

**2.** Use a skew chisel to form a spigot in the top of the lid about ⅜ in. long and about ½ in. to ⅝ in. in diameter. The spigot should be slightly larger on the end so that the spigot jaws will get a tight grip.

**USE A GOUGE** to begin shaping the topside of the lid. Then use a skew to form a spigot on top to hold it in the chuck.

# Hollow the inside of the lid

**A**

**USE A PENCIL** to mark the diameter of the inside of the lid.

**1.** Mount the lid in the spigot jaws and then use a pencil to mark the size of the base's rim on the face of the lid (**PHOTO A**). You will need to measure the diameter of the raised tongue on the base and then use that diameter to make your mark.

**2.** Use a gouge to hollow the inside of the lid. You must be very careful at this point to avoid a catch and to get a smooth cut (**PHOTO B**). Make certain that your gouge is sharp and that you have your tool carefully braced.

**3.** I work my way by trial and error toward a perfect fit. This requires stopping the lathe and checking the fit on the base and then removing slightly more until the lid snaps in place (**PHOTO C**).

USE A GOUGE to hollow the inside of the lid.

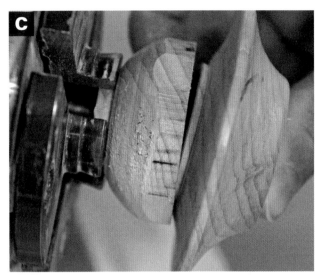

CHECK THE FIT of the base inside the underside of the lid. Widen the cut slightly until it just fits over the lip and snaps into place.

USE A SKEW CHISEL to finish rounding the lid, leaving just a bit of the stem at the top to keep the lid tightly in place.

**4.** Once the lid fits, I put the base back on the chuck and put the lid in place. Use a larger sharp skew chisel to round the top side of the lid while the live center in the tailstock of the lathe keeps the lid tightly in place. When you've achieved the shape you want, begin thinning the spigot on the lid until it is smaller than ¼ in. diameter so that it can be removed in step 6 **(PHOTO D )**.

USE SANDPAPER to polish the lid and remove any remaining tool marks.

**5.** Use various grits of sandpaper to polish the lid and remove any remaining tool marks. I start with 150-grit and work up to 320-grit **(PHOTO E)**.

**6.** Use duct tape or masking tape to secure the lid in place while you drill the hole for the turned pull **(PHOTO F)**. Use a ¼-in. drill in a drill chuck mounted in the tailstock to drill into the spigot. As you go deeper, the spigot will simply disappear and the drill will form the necessary hole for the turned pull.

USE DUCT TAPE or masking tape to hold the lid in place as you drill the hole in the top for the turned pull.

# Make a turned pull

**I CHOSE BLACK WALNUT FOR THIS PULL** and mounted a piece of it in the spigot jaws while using a live center in the tailstock to stabilize the other end.

**1.** With a small gouge, form a tapered cylinder with the narrow end at the tailstock. Then form a ¼-in. by ¼-in. tenon on the wide end. I use a parting tool for this operation, and check frequently with a dial caliper to see that I've not gone too deep. When the measurement shows ¼ in. I stop forming the tenon and proceed to shaping the rest of the pull **(PHOTO A)**.

**2.** Use pen-turning tools if you have them to shape the pull. Smaller tools will help, though the

**USE A PARTING TOOL** to form a tenon at the base of the turned lid pull. Keep reducing the size slightly until the caliper measures ¼ in.

**WITH THE TENON FORMED,** proceed to give the pull a shape you like. I use a set of small lathe chisels intended for turning pens to give the pull interesting detail.

first pulls I made were done with conventional tools. Use a small gouge to form cove cuts and a skew chisel to form corresponding beads. This is a chance for experiment and play. So have fun **(PHOTO B )**.

**3.** While it is still on the lathe, use sandpaper to sand and polish the pull. I start with 150-grit and stop when I reach 320-grit **(PHOTO C )**.

**4.** When the pull is finished, simply put a dab of glue in the hole drilled in the lid and push the pull into place. Make sure it is centered and stands straight up as the glue sets. It helps to observe from all angles.

**USE SANDPAPER** to sand and polish the pull while it is still on the lathe.

## A Box with Contrasting Wood

You can alter the design of this box in many ways. Different shapes may appeal to you, or you can mix and match woods. For instance, this mesquite box with maple lid and mesquite pull offers greater contrast than the box made with maple and walnut. You can also add additional detail to the base or lid of the box. The fine bead on this mesquite box was added with a skew chisel.

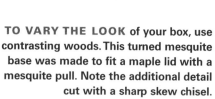

**TO VARY THE LOOK** of your box, use contrasting woods. This turned mesquite base was made to fit a maple lid with a mesquite pull. Note the additional detail cut with a sharp skew chisel.

## Cherry Cut-Out Box

You can also detail your box to add interest. This cherry box was altered by cutting half circles from the edges with a scrollsaw.

**ANOTHER DISTINCTIVE DESIGN** variation can be attained by cutting away parts of the base using a scrollsaw. Hold small half circles of card stock in place as you trace what is to be cut away.

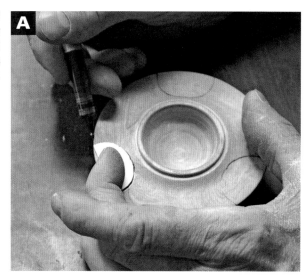

**1.** First cut a half circle from card stock and trace it on the top edge of the base **(PHOTO A )**.

**2.** Use a scrollsaw to cut the half circles from the base **(PHOTO B )**. Use a fine blade and keep a good grip on the base; a two-hand grip will help give greater control during this cut.

**3.** Use a spindle sander or large dowel wrapped in sandpaper to sand the cuts smooth **(PHOTO C )**.

**4.** Use a dowel wrapped in fine-grit sandpaper to finish the job **(PHOTO D )**.

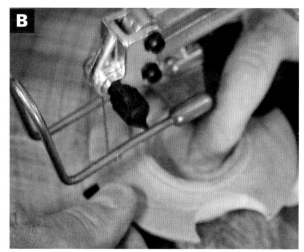

**USE THE SCROLLSAW** to make your cuts.

**USE A SPINDLE SANDER** to make the scrollsawn surfaces smooth to the eye and to the touch.

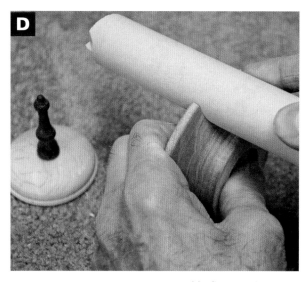

**USE A LARGE DOWEL** wrapped in fine sandpaper to polish the inside of the scrollsawn cuts.

# A Business Card Box

This simple and clever box serves as a pocket caddy for your business cards, keeping their edges crisp and unworn, and when open on your desk it serves as a dispenser, holding 15 cards ready to be dispersed to your clients and guests.

Making this box requires guides to assist with fitting the lid, but other than that it is created using basic boxmaking techniques. (For more information on boxmaking see my earlier books, *Taunton's Complete Illustrated Guide to Box Making*, *Basic Box Making*, and *Beautiful Boxes*, The Taunton Press, Inc.) Not all the steps are easy, but with some woodworking skill an intermediate-level boxmaker can make quick work of this box, and make a few extras for friends at the same time.

On this box, I used simple keyed miter joints for the front corners, a fixed panel on the back, and brass pin hinges to affix the lid. The contrasting keys add to the beauty of the box while also making it strong enough for years of use. The lid is designed to fold all the way back so that it can hold cards in a convenient position while the box is open.

With this box, you will need to make at least a pair of boxes at the same time in order to follow the steps described. Luckily this box makes a great gift, so the extra one can be put to good use.

# A business card box

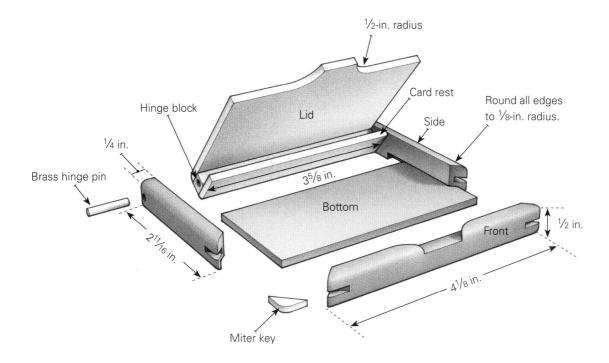

½-in. radius

Hinge block

Card rest

Lid

Side

Round all edges
to ⅛-in. radius.

¼ in.

Brass hinge pin

3⅝ in.

Bottom

Front

½ in.

2¹¹/₁₆ in.

4⅛ in.

Miter key

## MATERIALS

| QUANTITY | PART | MATERIAL | SIZE | NOTES |
|---|---|---|---|---|
| 2* | Fronts | Walnut | ¼ in. x ½ in. x 4⅛ in. | |
| 2* | Sides | Walnut | ¼ in. x ½ in x 5⅝ in. | Each side will be cut into two during the assembly process in order to make two boxes. |
| 2* | Bottoms | Walnut | ⅛ in. x 1³/₁₆ in. x 3⅞ in. | Use measurements from the actual box. |
| 1 | Lid | Maple | ⅛ in. x 2¹³/₁₆ in. x 3⅝ in. | |
| 1 | Hinge block | Maple | ¼ in. x ⁵/₁₆ in. x 3⅝ in. | |
| 1 | Card rest | Maple | ⅛ in. x ¹¹/₁₆ in. x 3⅝ in. | |
| 4 | Miter keys | Maple | ⅛ in. x ½ in. x 1 in. | Adjust the thickness of the keys to fit the sawkerf of the blade used to cut the key slots. |
| 2 | Hinge pins | Brass rod | ⅛ in. diameter x ⁵/₈ in. | Available from a hardware or welding supply store. |

*Makes two boxes. The rest of the materials list is for one box.

# Make the box frame

**1.** I begin by ripping and planing stock to thickness. I make sides and fronts for two boxes at the same time. The stock for these parts can be resawn from thicker stock in order to make the best use of the material. First rip the stock slightly oversize and then plane to the final dimensions.

**2.** Once the material has been planed to the right thickness and width, I use the tablesaw with a stop block on the miter sled to make certain that pairs of parts (fronts and sides) are cut to the required lengths **(PHOTO A )**. Using the miter sled and stop block miters the ends and cuts them to the required lengths at the same time. Note that when these parts are assembled and glued into a rectangular form, it's only so that they can be cut apart into two boxes later after the essential machining had been done, so two fronts and two sides will make two boxes. You will need to change the location of the stop block as you switch from cutting fronts to sides.

**3.** Spread glue on each mitered surface and clamp the box frame together securely while the glue sets **(PHOTO B )**.

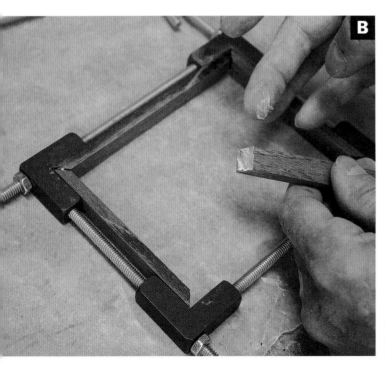

**GLUE THE BOX** sides and fronts into a single form, which will later become two boxes.

# Rabbet the box frame

**THE NEXT STEP IS A RATHER UNUSUAL ONE,** requiring a special router bit designed to cut an ⅛-in. rabbet in the edge of the stock for the box bottom. I use a rabbeting bit made by Amana Tool® (Amana MR0101), with a tiny ³⁄₁₆-in.-diameter bearing that allows it to rout deeply into corners. A larger bit would work but not fit as close, and would require a great deal more chisel work to square the corners.

**1.** To control the travel of the bearing on the inside of the glued frame and prevent a cut where the hinge pins will fit, I use a block of wood as a spacer block. For this project, my spacer is a Baltic birch block that is ½ in. by 3⅝ in. by 3½ in. This guides the router bit and keeps it from routing the full inside length of the sides. I leave the clamp securing the corners of the frame in place to give

the joints greater strength. Rout with the spacer block on one side with the height of the router bit set ⅛ in. from the top of the router table **(PHOTO A )**.

**2.** Move the spacer block to the other side and continue the routing operation. The bearing will follow the block of wood and will be prevented from routing the full length of the sides **(PHOTO B )**. With the sides turned upside down and with the block of wood removed, you can see the results on p. 128 **(PHOTO C )**. The rabbet when finished should fit the box bottom described in the materials list. If your spacer block is the correct size, you use the right router bit, and your box sides are the right length, it will. But to allow for any possible errors, cut the box bottom after the routing and chiseling are complete.

**USE A RABBETING BIT** in the router table to rout the space for the box bottom to fit. The spacer block restricts the length of the cut, keeping it away from the place where the hinge pins will fit.

**MOVE THE SPACER** block to the other side as you rout for the other box bottom to fit.

**3.** Use a chisel to square the inside corners of the frame so that a fixed hardwood bottom can be glued in place on each side. The routed side of the wooden block at the center helps to locate the chisel cuts on either side of the box (**PHOTO D**).

**THE RABBET IS CAREFULLY FORMED** in just the right places.

**CHISEL THE ROUNDED CORNERS SQUARE.** Use the spacer block to provide alignment for the chisel's cut along the box sides.

D

# Fit the miter keys

**ONE SIMPLE WAY TO STRENGTHEN AND** decorate the corners of a box is with contrasting keys that fit in slots cut in the mitered corners. I cut the grooves for these keys on the tablesaw using a simple guide that holds the frame corners upright at a 45-degree angle (see the sidebar on p. 130).

**1.** Set the tablesaw blade height at about 3/8 in. so that it will not cut all the way into the interior of the box. You can use a standard ripping blade for this cut, but I chose a thin-kerf blade so the keys would be slightly thinner than those used on a larger box. I use a guide that slides along the

**CUT MITER KEY SLOTS** at each corner of the box frame.

**WHEN RIPPING THIN STRIPS** for making miter keys, check the thickness of the stock by fitting it in the saw kerf from the blade used for the key slots.

fence while two supports hold the box parts at a 45-degree angle. I hold a block of wood at the side to keep the box parts in the guide and to hold the guide tightly against the fence at the same time **(PHOTO A )**. Push the box and guide through the cut and then back before cutting the next corner.

**2.** Cut thin strips of miter key stock on the tablesaw to fit in the key slots. You will need to go by fit, and not by the actual measure of the thickness of the stock, as they must not be too loose or too tight. If they are too loose they will fall out. If they are too tight, you will need to hammer them into place and will likely break the mitered corners loose. To make sure that the key stock fits the grooves, I create a test block by cutting partway into the end of a block of wood. I use the same blade used to cut the keyed miter slots, but I stop and pull the block back from the blade after cutting only partway in. I can then rip a strip and check to see how it fits the cut. If it's loose or tight, I adjust the fence on the saw to rip a better-fitting strip **(PHOTO B )**.

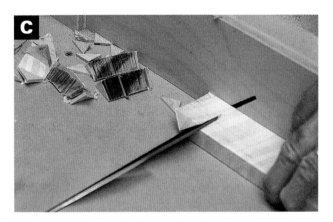

**BUNDLE THE KEY STOCK STRIPS** with tape and cut them using the miter sled on the tablesaw.

**3.** To cut the keys into triangles, I wrap a number of strips together with tape so that I can cut them using the 45-degree sled on the tablesaw. Without the tape, these will fly about dangerously as they are cut. The tape wrapped securely around the bundle of strips holds the loose keys together and keeps you safe **(PHOTO C )**. After they are cut, the keys should be oversize in width and length so that they can be sanded flush with the box sides in a later step.

**4.** Glue the contrasting keys in the miter key slots. I first test a key in a slot to make certain it will fit well without having to apply force. Then I spread just a bit of glue on each key. Don't worry if the keys stick out a ways at this point, as they will be trimmed flush in a later step **(PHOTO D )**.

**GLUE CONTRASTING KEYS** in the miter key slots.

## MAKE A KEYED MITER GUIDE

Contrasting miters strengthen and decorate the corners of this box. In order to cut the slots for the miters I build this simple and quick-to-make guide to hold the box vertically at a 45-degree angle. It slides along the fence as you hold the box in place. The same pressure used to hold the box in

the guide also holds the guide tightly to the fence of the saw as you move it through the cut.

Making it is easy. A piece of Baltic birch or other plywood at least ½ in. thick serves as the part that slides along the fence and holds the box in a vertical position. Use another piece of

Baltic birch plywood to build the cradle that will hold the box at the correct angle (45 degrees) throughout the cut. This second piece of plywood is cut at a 45-degree angle. Then one of the cut pieces is flipped over to form the cradle. These two cut pieces are screwed to the first piece.

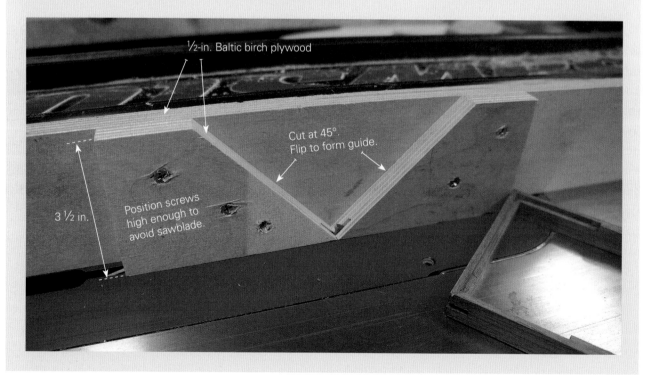

½-in. Baltic birch plywood

Cut at 45°. Flip to form guide.

3 ½ in.

Position screws high enough to avoid sawblade.

# Prepare the stock for the bottoms and lid

**THE BOTTOMS AND LID REQUIRE THIN CUT** stock. In fact, the wood is so thin that many planers will have difficulty providing you with the right size stock. One solution is to rip the stock slightly oversize in thickness and then run it through a drum sander until it is ⅛ in. thick. Another solution is to just rip it to the correct thickness on the tablesaw, and then plan to sand the parts flush after assembly. In either case, some careful sawing is required. Use a push block to safely control the stock through the cut.

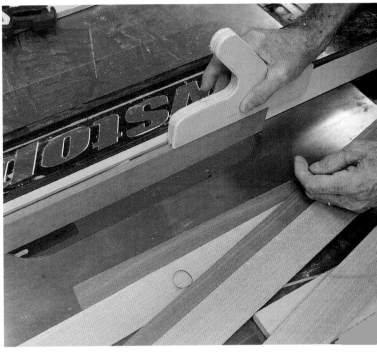

**USE THE TABLESAW** to rip stock for the box bottoms and lid.

# Install the bottoms

**1.** From the stock you just cut in the last step, cut the bottom pieces to fit the bottom of the box. I use the tablesaw to rip the stock to width and then the crosscut sled on the tablesaw to cut the parts to length. Check the fit before you apply glue. The square corners of the box bottoms should fit into the corners you cut square with a chisel earlier. Some additional chiseling may be required before you glue them in place.

**2.** When they fit properly, glue the box bottoms into the box frame (**PHOTO A**).

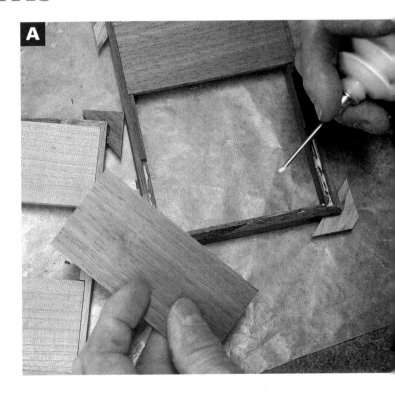

**GLUE THE BOX BOTTOMS** in place. A small squeeze bottle helps to apply just the right amount of glue.

CLAMP THE BOTTOMS
in place as the glue sets.

**3.** Use clamps to hold the box bottoms in place as the glue sets (**PHOTO B**). The advantage of making more than one box at a time is that the box sides will be held in perfect relationship to each other while the bottom is glued in place.

**4.** Having the keys and bottom in place will make the box assembly strong enough for the rest of our boxmaking steps. Use a bandsaw to cut the keys almost flush to the box sides. Leave a small amount of key to be sanded flush later (**PHOTO C**). Note in the photo at left how I've made a cut in the low fence clamped to the bandsaw table. This allows the box to slide along the fence with the blade only able to cut the keys and not the box sides.

TRIM THE MITER KEYS nearly flush with the box sides, leaving a small amount of key protruding to be sanded flush later.

# Fit the lid

**FITTING THE LID TO THE BOX REQUIRES** making two guides, one for the lid and the other for the body of the box.

**1.** Rip the lid stock to the width described in the materials list. Cut the lid to the length required to fit the inside of the box, using either the crosscut sled on the tablesaw or the compound miter saw. Also cut the rest of the lid parts (the card rest and hinge block) as described in the materials list; these must be cut to the exact same length as the lid.

**2.** The lid for this box has a lift tab that extends beyond the front edge of the box. To shape the front edge of the lid you'll need to make guides for routing both the box and lid. See the sidebar on pp. 134–135 for directions on making these guides.

**3.** To shape the front of the lid, set the lid routing guide in place over the lid and rout using a ½-in.-diameter dado clean-out bit. This bit has a bearing atop the cutter and follows the guide to replicate its exact shape on the wood held securely underneath **(PHOTO A)**.

**4.** Clamp the box to the workbench, put the box front routing guide in place on the front of the box, and rout with the dado clean-out bit set so that the depth of the cut into the box equals the thickness of the lid. Rout one side and then the opposite side to form the front edges of two boxes. A laminate trimmer is the best tool for this, as a larger router would interfere with the clamp used to secure the box to the workbench **(PHOTO B)**.

**A ½-IN. DADO** clean-out bit in the laminate trimmer follows the guide and reproduces the guide's shape in the lid.

**USE A LAMINATE TRIMMER** and dado clean-out bit to follow the guide and rout the front of the box.

## Lid Routing Guides

### Lid routing guide

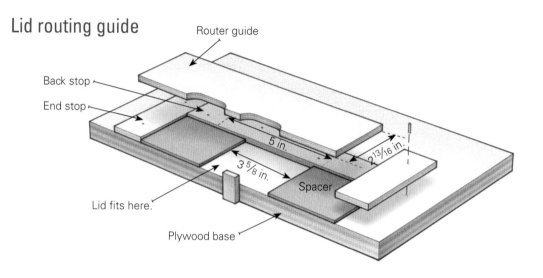

Router guide

Back stop

End stop

5 in.

$2^{13}/16$ in.

$3^{5}/8$ in.

Spacer

Lid fits here.

Plywood base

### Box front routing guide

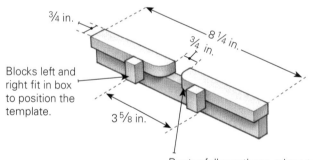

$3/4$ in.

$8^{1}/4$ in.

$3/4$ in.

Blocks left and right fit in box to position the template.

$3^{5}/8$ in.

Router follows these edges to rout the inside of the box to fit the lid.

## Make the lid routing guide

**1.** I use a 1-in.-diameter router bit in the router table to make a cut equidistant from the two ends of a ¼-in.-thick piece of Baltic birch. Moving between stops, rout a recess about 2 in. long on both sides of the center of the stock, leaving a piece ¾ in. long undisturbed at the center. To make this guide piece requires only one setup, as the stock is simply flipped over to form the opposite side **(PHOTO A)**.

**2.** Use 1½-in.-wide strips of Baltic birch plywood to build a tightly fitting frame around the guide you formed on the router table. I used a piece of scrap ¾-in. plywood as the base. Then cut pieces of thin stock to fit on each side of the lid. These should be equal in thickness to the lid and equal in length, so that they will hold the lid stock exactly centered in the guide **(PHOTO B)**.

**MAKE A ROUTING GUIDE** for the front of the box lids.

**A LAMINATE TRIMMER** will follow the lid routing guide to form the shape of the lid.

## Make the box front routing guide

**1.** To make the guide for routing the front edge of the box, first round two pieces of hardwood, ¾ in. wide by ⁷⁄₁₆ in. thick, to a radius of ½ in. **(PHOTO A)**.

Hold the two pieces together so that they can be rounded on a disk sander at the same time, and compare them to a routed box lid to see that you've established the right curve.

**2.** Glue the rounded parts to another piece of ⁷⁄₁₆-in.-thick hardwood. I made mine on a strip of hardwood 8¼ in. long and used the lid guide to see that they were glued with just the right spacing between **(PHOTO B)**.

**3.** Next, glue blocks on the inside of the guide to hold it in the right position on the box. This will take careful measuring to make certain that the guide is exactly centered on the front of the box **(PHOTO C)**.

**ROUND THE PARTS** of the routing guide for the box body using a disk sander. The radius should conform to the shape of the lid.

**AS YOU ASSEMBLE** the guide for routing the front of the box, check the position of its parts by comparing it with the routing guide for the lid.

**THE GUIDE MUST BE EXACTLY** centered on the front of the box.

USE THE SLED on the tablesaw to cut the original box body assembly into two parts. A small amount of waste will be left.

# Cut the boxes apart and make two from one

**USE A 90-DEGREE SLED ON THE TABLESAW** to cut the framed box body in two. Use a stop block to establish the position of the cut and to ensure that the cut on each side is exactly the same. Note that I've added enough material to the length of the box sides so that each box will need to be cut again to remove the small amount of waste stock.

# Assemble and install the lid

**1.** Use glue and clamps to assemble the parts of the lid, consisting of the card rest, the hinge block, and the lid. I lay a small bead of glue down the length of each part using a squeeze bottle, and carefully align the parts at the ends and along the sides to make sure they line up. Do not simply glue and walk away immediately. Sometimes parts slide in response to clamping pressure and will need a bit more attention to alignment than you expect. When you are satisfied that the alignment of the parts is near perfect, leave the parts clamped for at least 45 minutes **(PHOTO A)**.

USE GLUE AND CLAMPS to assemble the parts for the box lid.

During glue-up it's always a good idea to check the alignment of your parts more than once, as parts can slide in relation to each other as clamping pressure is applied.

**2.** Use the lid drilling guide for the drill press, as illustrated on p. 30, to drill ⅛-in.-diameter holes through the box sides and into the lid on each side for the brass hinge pins (**PHOTO B**).

**3.** I cut the brass hinge pins from a ⅛-in.-diameter brass rod using a large wire cutter and then gently sand one end smooth before driving it into place (**PHOTO C**).

**4.** Rout all the edges of the box, except for the lift tab left on the lid top, using a ⅛-in.-radius roundover bit on the router table. The lift tab can be lightly hand-sanded to a smooth contour.

**5.** I begin sanding on the stationary belt sander and then use a random-orbit sander with 150-grit, 240-grit, and 320-grit before applying a wipe-on Danish oil finish.

**DRILL THE HOLES** for the brass pin hinges.

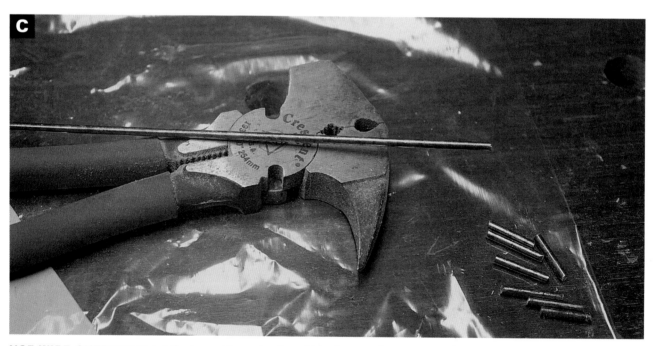

**USE WIRE CUTTERS** to cut the brass hinge pins from ⅛-in. brass rod.

# Add inlay

**CONSIDER USING STOCK INLAY TO**
decorate your box, as I did. On this box I added inlay on both the front and the back, so that when the box is open to put the cards on display, the inlay makes a bold statement of quality workmanship.

I routed grooves on both the front and back for the inlay **(PHOTO A )**. Use cauls to clamp the inlay in place as the glue sets **(PHOTO B )**. To create your own inlay, see the Hinged Pocket Box chapter.

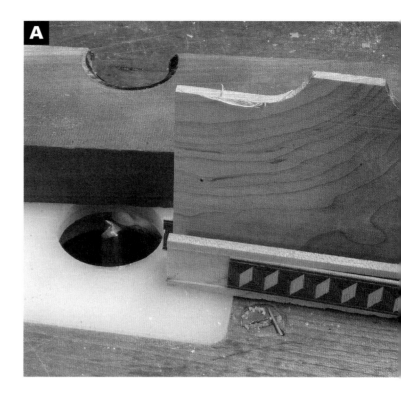

**USE THE ROUTER TABLE** to rout a groove for the stock inlay.

**USE CAULS** to distribute clamping pressure as the inlay is glued in place.

## DESIGN OPTIONS

**One of the great ways to make your card box unique is by varying the species and color of the woods used. You may do the entire card box in a single color of wood or choose contrasting woods to make your box stand out and get more attention. If you opt to use a contrasting color for the lid, choose that same species for the contrasting keys that secure the corners.**

Some of my favorite woods are the ones that I find growing in my own neighborhood, like the walnut, cherry, and maple woods used to make these card boxes. They may not be as glamorous as some I might make from more exotic woods, but they offer me the comfort of knowing that the very same woods will be available for future generations, not just my own.

The wood combinations shown above are walnut with cherry, maple with walnut, maple with cherry, and walnut with cherry again. Feel free to experiment with your own choices of colors and woods.

# A Japanese Puzzle Box

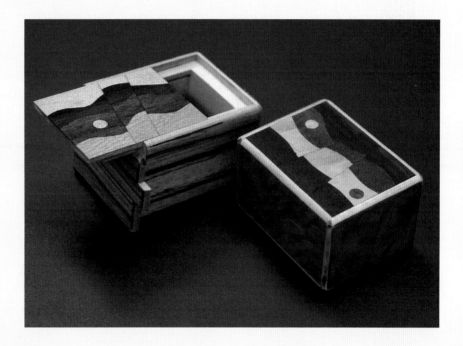

Japanese boxmakers have made puzzle boxes for over a century that have been carried home by tourists from all over the world. The user must solve the puzzle by sliding pieces around in the correct order to open the lid. Japanese puzzle boxes are made with intricate veneer patterns, and the craftsmanship is exquisite. The simple ones require seven steps to gain access to the interior of the box, and the mechanism that allows them to work is completely hidden from view.

I first became interested in making these boxes when the school where I teach hosted an exchange student from Japan, and it was a disappointment to both of us that I could not instruct her on how they were made. I began experimenting a bit at that point but quickly gave up.

Finally, in writing a book about tiny boxes, I realized that this book would not be complete without attempting to make one of the most interesting and famous tiny boxes of all. In order to understand how the mechanism in a Japanese puzzle box works, I used a small bandsaw to cut one open, and then proceeded to reverse engineer the necessary small parts.

I left this chapter till the end of the book due to the complexity of the procedures involved. I do not consider this a box suitable for beginning boxmakers, and offer it here in the hopes that others will be inspired to experiment and learn from the process. I offer this disclaimer: I am a beginner in the making of Japanese puzzle boxes.

The techniques I have used are not exactly those used in Japan. The making of this box relies upon techniques that would be more familiar to Western woodworkers. Also, the veneer patterns Japanese boxmakers use are a well-practiced art and are beyond the scope of this book. I have used thicker veneers with simpler patterns. In any case, I hope you enjoy the making of a Japanese puzzle box.

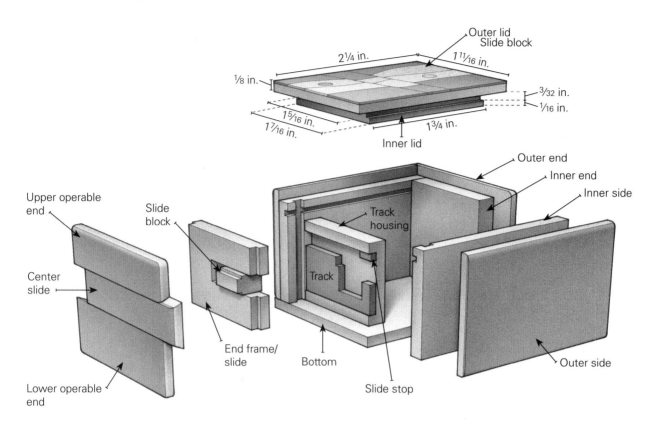

Outer lid
Slide block
2¼ in.
1 ¹¹/₁₆ in.
⅛ in.
³/₃₂ in.
¹/₁₆ in.
1 ⁵/₁₆ in.
1 ⁷/₁₆ in.
1 ¾ in.
Inner lid

Upper operable end
Slide block
Outer end
Inner end
Inner side
Center slide
Track housing
Track
End frame/ slide
Bottom
Outer side
Lower operable end
Slide stop

**THESE ARE THE SEVEN STEPS** required to open the puzzle box. Here you can see the slide block making its way through the hidden track formed by the track housing, slide stop, and track. The final step moves the operable end low enough to allow the lid to slide open. We'll cover this in greater detail later in the chapter.

# Puzzle box mechanism

**4** Upper operable end

**2** Slide block

**3** End frame/slide

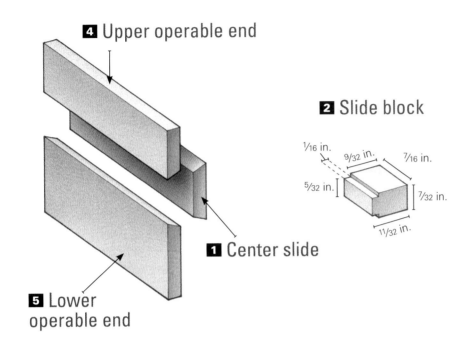

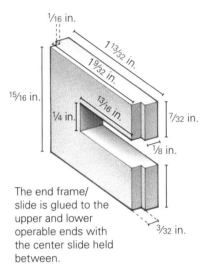

**1** Center slide

**5** Lower operable end

1/16 in.

9/32 in.

7/16 in.

5/32 in.

7/32 in.

11/32 in.

1/16 in.

1 13/32 in.

19/32 in.

15/16 in.

13/16 in.

1/4 in.

7/32 in.

1/8 in.

3/32 in.

The end frame/slide is glued to the upper and lower operable ends with the center slide held between.

**7** Track       **8** Slide stop

**6** Track housing

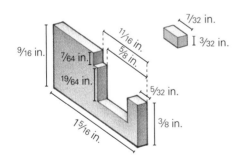

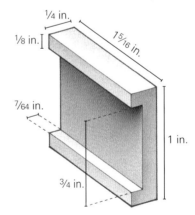

7/32 in.

I 3/32 in.

11/16 in.

9/16 in.   7/64 in.   5/8 in.

19/64 in.

5/32 in.

3/8 in.

1 5/16 in.

1/4 in.

1/8 in.

1 5/16 in.

7/64 in.

1 in.

3/4 in.

# MATERIALS

| QUANTITY | PART | MATERIAL | SIZE | NOTES |
|---|---|---|---|---|
| **Puzzle Mechanism** | | | | |
| 1* | Upper operable end* | Basswood | $\frac{1}{8}$ in. × $\frac{7}{16}$ in. × $1\frac{15}{16}$ in. | |
| 1 | Center slide* | Basswood | $\frac{1}{8}$ in. × $\frac{1}{2}$ in. × $1\frac{15}{16}$ in. | |
| 1 | Lower operable end* | Basswood | $\frac{1}{8}$ in. × $\frac{3}{4}$ in. × $1\frac{15}{16}$ in. | |
| 1 | Track housing | Basswood | $\frac{1}{4}$ in. × 1 in. × $1\frac{5}{16}$ in. | |
| 1 | Track | Poplar | $\frac{5}{64}$ in. × $1\frac{5}{16}$ in. × $\frac{9}{16}$ in. | The final track thickness will be $\frac{3}{32}$ in. |
| 1 | Slide stop | Poplar | $\frac{5}{64}$ in. × $\frac{3}{32}$ in. × $\frac{7}{32}$ in. | |
| 1 | End frame/slide | Basswood | $\frac{7}{32}$ in. × $\frac{15}{16}$ in. × $1\frac{13}{32}$ in. | |
| 1 | Slide block | Basswood | $\frac{7}{32}$ in. × $\frac{11}{32}$ in. × $\frac{7}{16}$ in. | |
| **Box Body** | | | | |
| 2 | Outer sides* | Basswood | $\frac{1}{8}$ in. × $1\frac{3}{8}$ in. × $2\frac{1}{4}$ in. | These pieces should initially be cut larger and will later be cut down to size. |
| 1 | Outer end* | Basswood | $\frac{1}{8}$ in. × $1\frac{1}{2}$ in. × $1\frac{15}{16}$ in. | |
| 1 | Bottom* | Basswood | $\frac{1}{8}$ in. × $1\frac{15}{16}$ in. × $2\frac{1}{4}$ in. | |
| 2 | Inner sides | Basswood | $\frac{3}{16}$ in. × $1\frac{1}{4}$ in. × $2\frac{1}{4}$ in. | |
| 1 | Inner end | Basswood | $\frac{1}{4}$ in. × $1\frac{1}{4}$ in. × $1\frac{5}{16}$ in. | |
| 1 | Inner lid | Basswood | $\frac{5}{32}$ in. × $1\frac{7}{16}$ in. × $1\frac{3}{4}$ in. | |
| 1 | Outer lid** | Basswood | $\frac{1}{8}$ in. × $1\frac{11}{16}$ in. × $2\frac{1}{4}$ in. | |
| 1 | Veneer | | $\frac{1}{32}$ in. × $2\frac{1}{8}$ in. × $11\frac{1}{2}$ in. | In addition, several layers of 3-in. × 4-in. veneer will be needed to use the mix-and-match veneering technique for the lid. |

**Note:** A single of piece of $\frac{1}{8}$ in. × $2\frac{1}{8}$ in. × $11\frac{1}{2}$ in. basswood will serve for the preliminary stock for all of the outer pieces except for the lid. The parts can be cut from this piece after the veneer is glued in place.

*All of these parts are to be veneered and can be cut from a single piece of veneered stock.

**Assemble veneer pattern to fit stock $\frac{1}{8}$ in. × 2 in. × $2\frac{1}{2}$ in., then trim to final size.

# How the box works

**TO UNDERSTAND HOW A JAPANESE PUZZLE** box is made and how it works, I took a small one that I had bought online and made cuts into the sides and bottom using a bandsaw, cutting just deep enough that it would come apart. I learned that the box was made in a series of layers, with the outermost layer being veneer. Next comes the material to which the veneer is glued, and then beneath that is the basic structure of the box, consisting of ends, sides, bottom, and lid.

The mechanism I discovered is surprisingly simple but requires some careful study. Each of the parts identified here is shown in the drawing on p. 143 and numbered for your reference. This is how it works: A thin piece of veneered wood at one end of the box, the center slide **1**, has a sliding dovetail

shape that allows it to slide back and forth between the upper **4** and lower **5** operable end parts, which are veneered in the same manner. In addition, the whole operable end of the box is attached to a piece that I've called the end frame/slide **3**, which is able to slide up and down in a track formed in the sides of the box. A small block of wood, the slide block **2**, is glued to the back of the center slide. The slide block and connected center slide move back and forth and up and down to follow a path formed by the track. The track housing **6** hides the track from view, and along with the track **7** and slide stop **8** establishes a range of motion for the slide block, allowing it to move only along a pattern of steps. The slide block can only slide side to side confined by a groove cut in the end frame/slide. The end frame/slide is glued to both the upper and lower operable end pieces with the center slide held between. As the center slide is moved back and forth, the slide block follows the track and allows the entire operable end to slide down in increments, following a groove cut in the box sides.

It takes seven steps to open the box (for more on these steps, see p. 167). The first six steps move the operable end low enough for the lid to pass over and must be completed in order. The seventh step is sliding the lid open. The real secret of the Japanese puzzle box is the hidden track. It allows the center slide to move back and forth and the operable end to move down, providing clearance for the lid to slide open. This is kind of a challenge to understand, I know, but once we get deeper into the making of the box it should become clearer. The photo on p. 142 demonstrates the internal process for opening or closing the box.

**CAREFUL BANDSAW CUTS** reveal the secrets of a Japanese puzzle box. A small block of wood attached to a sliding dovetailed piece moves right and left along a track, allowing the end of the box to move down in steps and out of the way of the sliding lid. Seven steps are required to open the box.

# Form the parts for the mechanism

**THIS BOX REQUIRES A GREAT DEAL OF** accuracy and that you follow the steps exactly as given. Please refer to the drawing and carefully check that each cut has been made correctly.

## Make the track housing

The track housing both houses and hides the track on the inside of the box. This part forms one end of the interior of the box, serves as part of the track for the sliding block, and also conceals the mechanism from view.

**1.** Cut the stock for the track housing to thickness and width but not to length.

**2.** Use a straight-cut router bit in the router table to rout a $7/64$-in.- (almost $1/8$-in.-) deep channel in the track housing. Working with a longer piece of stock than is necessary to make one box adds a margin of safety to the operation.

**USE THE ROUTER TABLE** to rout the track housing. To do this safely I work with a longer strip than needed, which also allows me to make parts for several boxes at the same time.

## Make the track

The track hidden inside the box is given its shape through a series of cuts on the tablesaw. I work with thicker stock and then cut it thin so that it can be glued in the track housing. This part of the box displays a particular genius, in that making this part is much easier than it would be to chisel a recess in solid wood for the mechanism to work.

**1.** Use the tablesaw to make the track. Make the first cut at the end of the stock, with a stop block controlling the position of the cut. This requires careful setting of the blade height and equal attention to the location of the stop block. For the first cut the stop block should be $11/16$ in. from the blade, with the blade height set at $3/16$ in. Note that

BEGIN FORMING THE TRACK using the tablesaw sled. This is the first of several necessary cuts. Note the space between the workpiece and stop block. This allows two cuts to be made, forming a wider cut.

**A**

ADJUST THE STOP BLOCK and depth of cut to continue forming the shape of the track.

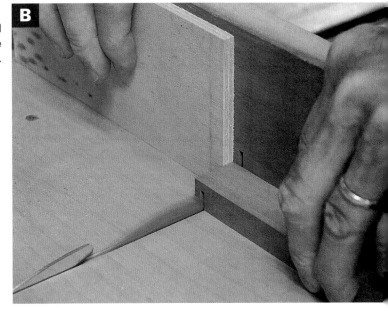

**B**

the track is cut upside down on the tablesaw sled. Following the dimensions in the drawing on p. 143, raise or lower the blade height and set the stop block position to make the required cuts (**PHOTO A**).

**2.** Cut a deeper and wider recess in the track stock next. This will involve both a change of blade height and a change of distance between the blade and stop block. Carefully set the stop block and tablesaw to form one side of the recess, make this cut, and then move the stop block to the second position and make a series of cuts to level the recess between the two outer cuts (**PHOTO B**). To make the best use of the stock, I make several track pieces at a time and have extras in case one or more break during cutting or handling (**PHOTO C**).

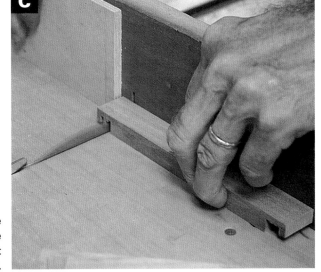

**C**

MOVE THE STOP BLOCK over for the next cut and then nibble away the space between. The completed cut can be seen at the opposite end of the stock.

**3.** There are two reasons why we cut the track thicker to start. One, it allows for a safer cut, and two, because these parts can be rather fragile before they are glued in the track housing, cutting them one at a time would cause them to break. Use the tablesaw to cut the track stock into thinner lengths. I aim for about 1/32 in. thinner than 1/8 in., so it will fit in the channel cut in the track housing (**PHOTO D**).

**4.** Tape the tracks together in a stack after you've sawn them to thickness. This will allow you to cut them to their finished length several at a time, without having them chewed and thrown by the saw (**PHOTO E**). Again, use the materials list on p. 144 to guide your cuts. And even if you are making only one box, you will find it best to work from larger stock and cut several at the same time. You will not regret having a spare.

**USE THE TABLESAW** to rip the track stock into thin strips. Tracks for several boxes can come from this operation.

**TO SAFELY CUT THE TRACKS** to length, first tape them together so they can be held to the sled and won't be sent flying from the impact of the saw. Use a stop block to control the length of the pieces and a hold-down stick to keep your hands a safe distance from the blade.

# Make the end frame/slide

Now that we've cut the track, it's time to move on to the end frame/slide, which is glued to both the upper and lower operable end pieces with the center slide held between. The end frame/slide has a groove that confines the path of the slide block, allowing it to slide only side to side. And it is also the piece that slides up and down in a track formed in the sides of the box.

**1.** Cut the stock for the end frame/slide to thickness and width but not to length, using the dimensions from the materials list and drawing.

**2.** Use the sled on the tablesaw to cut the side-to-side groove on the end frame/slide. Again, use the materials list and drawing for the exact location of the groove. Raise the blade to cut the length of the groove in two steps. The two cuts are necessary to create a wide-enough cut. First make one cut $^{57}/_{64}$ in. deep, with the fence set so that the first cut will be $^{25}/_{64}$ in. from the edge of the stock **(PHOTO A )**. Then move the stop block $^{1}/_{8}$ in. before making a second cut. The width of the resulting groove should be $^{1}/_{4}$ in. **(PHOTO B )**. Note that I am making these cuts at each end of the stock, thus forming two slide parts from a single setup. Even if you are making only one box, it is safer to work with greater lengths of stock, as the size of this part would make safe cutting difficult.

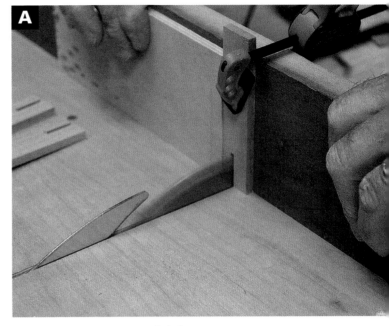

**USE THE TABLESAW** and sled to cut a groove into the end of the end frame/slide. Use a stop block clamped to the sled to control the position of the stock and use a clamp to hold the piece to the sled to keep your fingers safe.

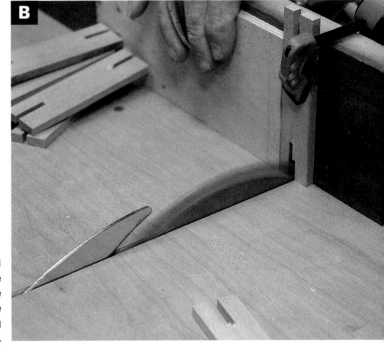

**CHANGE THE POSITION** of the stop block for the second cut. Note that the stock is long enough to make this cut at both ends, forming parts for two boxes.

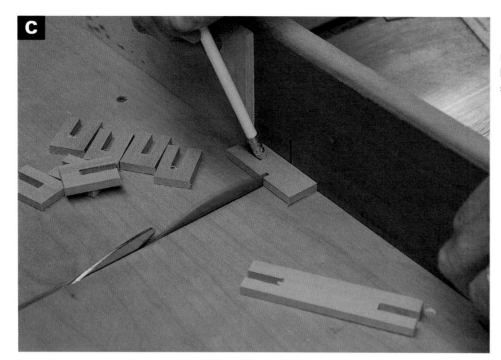

**USE THE SLED** and stop block to cut the end/frame slide to its finished length.

**D**

**USE THE TABLESAW** to form a small tongue at each end of the end frame/side. A zero-clearance insert is required to support the stock through this cut, and a shopmade push block is necessary to keep the fingers a safe distance away. Note the tongues on the already complete parts in the foreground.

**3.** Use the sled on the tablesaw to cut the end frame/slide to its finished length (**PHOTO C**).

**4.** Form a small tongue on each side of the end frame/slide that will slide in a groove to be cut in the box sides. I do this on the tablesaw with the distance between the blade and fence set to form the thickness of the tongue and the height of the tablesaw blade set to form its length. A zero-clearance insert is required to support the stock. Use a push block to guide the part safely through the cut and to keep your fingers a safe distance from the blade (**PHOTO D**). It's useful to have extra parts available for practice cuts to make sure that the final dimensions of this part conform to the dimensions given in the drawing and materials list.

Now that you've completed what may be the most difficult part of making a Japanese puzzle box, we can get on to making the box itself. We will finish making the rest of the mechanism parts in a later step.

# Cut and veneer the box sides, ends, and bottom

**WE WILL START MAKING THE BOX BY** cutting the parts for the sides, ends, and bottom first. As with the Japanese versions of this box, the sides, ends, and bottom are built in layers, and I apply the veneers first.

**1.** Cut stock ⅛ in. thick for the outer sides, bottom, and outer ends (which include the center slide and operable end pieces). It is easiest to veneer all these pieces at the same time.

**2.** Glue the veneers to the outer pieces you just cut (**PHOTO A**). I use carpenter's glue and then I stack alternating layers of glued-up veneer and stock so that multiple pieces can be glued at the same time between cauls. The cauls help to spread the pressure from the C-clamps so that it is evenly applied. A piece of waxed paper between the veneers stacked face to face prevents them from becoming stuck to each other (**PHOTO B**). You can glue up enough veneered wood at a time to make more than one box (**PHOTO C**).

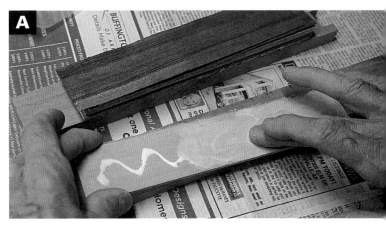

**GLUE VENEERS** to ⅛-in. stock to begin forming the outside layer of the box. I work with stock of sufficient length and width to form the sides, ends, and bottom of the box in a single operation.

**USE CAULS AND C-CLAMPS** to press the veneer tightly in place as the glue sets. Waxed paper keeps the veneer from sticking to the cauls and allows several pieces to be glued and clamped at the same time.

## WORK SMART

When preparing matching veneered parts, cut your stock just wider than will be needed for the widest part.

**THESE ARE THE VENEERED PARTS** for the outsides of four boxes.

# Make a patterned veneer lid

**THE COMPLEX VENEER PATTERNS USED IN** the Japanese puzzle boxes could, as I said, take a lifetime of work to perfect, so I opted for a simple process in which veneers are cut while stacked and then rearranged in a mix-and-match veneering technique.

**1.** First, stack three pieces of veneer in various colors and tape them together on the edges **(PHOTO A )**. This will hold them together as scroll-saw cuts divide them into parts. You can use more colors if you like, but three seems to work out just right for this size box.

**TO BEGIN MAKING** the patterned veneer lid, make sandwiches of stacked veneers. Tape the edges so that they hold together in reference to each other.

**2.** Make a series of meandering cuts with a scroll-saw with a fine-cut blade, but avoid overly complex curves, as these will be difficult to pull together tightly enough to hide the saw kerf **(PHOTO B )**.

**3.** After removing the tape, the pieces can be rearranged into as many different assemblies as there were layers in the original stack **(PHOTO C )**.

**4.** Once you've created a veneer pattern you like, use tape to begin pulling the pieces tightly together into a single piece **(PHOTO D )**.

**5.** To add variation to the pattern, I use a paper cutter to cut the assembled veneer into additional parts **(PHOTO E )**. When these pieces are taped back together slightly offset, it makes an interesting pattern **(PHOTO F )**. Use a paper punch to add even more interest. I punch a hole and then fill the hole with a piece of veneer punched from contrasting wood **(PHOTO G )**.

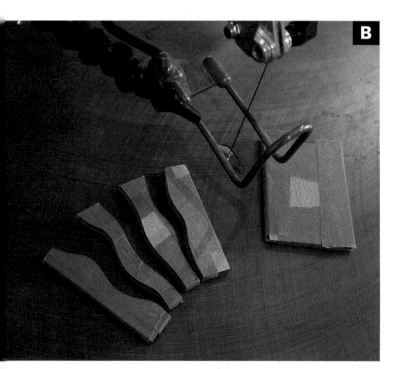

**MAKE A SERIES** of wandering scrollsaw cuts to begin forming your pattern.

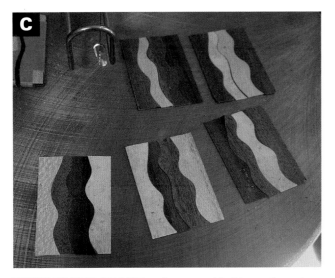

**WHEN TAKEN APART** and reassembled in a mix-and-match manner, interesting patterns can be formed.

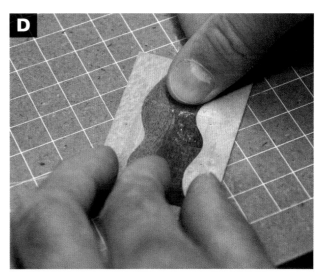

**USE CLEAR TAPE** to hold the pieces of veneer tightly together.

**USE A PAPER CUTTER** to cut the assembled veneer pieces into additional parts. A very sharp knife could also be used for this.

**OFFSET THE PARTS** and reassemble them in a more interesting and dynamic pattern. Use clear tape so you can see the results from both sides.

**USE A PAPER PUNCH** to make holes of contrasting veneer to create focal points in your design.

**6.** Spread glue on the ⅛-in.-thick outer lid stock and glue the veneer to it to form the decorative panel for the top of the puzzle box **(PHOTO H)**. I want this stock and veneer to be larger than the planned finished size of the lid. Use cauls and C-clamps to hold the veneer in place as the glue dries. Waxed paper can help ensure that the veneered panel does not stick to the caul **(PHOTO I)**.

**SPREAD GLUE** on the ⅛-in.-thick lid stock and glue the veneer to it.

**USE CAULS, C-CLAMPS, AND WAXED PAPER** to hold the veneer securely to the underlying stock as the glue sets.

# Form the inner box sides

**THE SIDES OF THIS BOX ARE BUILT UP IN** layers, with the inner sides housing the mechanism and the outer sides adding the beautiful veneer. The inner box sides must be grooved for the sliding lid to fit, and also for the end frame/slide that allows the end to move down to provide clearance for the lid to open.

**1.** Prepare the stock for the inner sides by first planing it to thickness and ripping it to width. Then use a sled on the tablesaw to cut the inner sides to length **(PHOTO A )**.

**2.** Switch to the router table and use a ¹⁄₁₆-in. router bit to rout the groove for the lid in the top of the inner box sides. Careful setup for this operation is required. I use a zero-clearance cover over the router table to give full support to the stock and also to make measuring the setup more precise **(PHOTO B )**. The two sides must be done in pairs.

**A**

USE THE SLED and a stop block to cut the inner sides to length on the tablesaw. The eraser end of a pencil keeps your hands a safe distance from the blade.

## WORK SMART

I use a zero-clearance cover, which is simply a piece of ⅛-in. Baltic birch plywood laid over the top surface of the router table with the fence positioned on top. The advantage of this setup is that with the router bit raised through, measuring is far easier than if you were trying to measure a small bit in a large opening.

**B**

USE A ¹⁄₁₆-IN. ROUTER BIT to form the tracks in the box sides for the lid to slide. A thin piece of plywood held down under the fence and over the opening of the router table provides zero clearance, and helps me more accurately set up my cut.

ROUT THE ENDS of the box sides. This was the first cut and the groove must be widened to fit the tongues on the end frame/slide. Please note that these parts, left and right, must be mirrors of each other, and that careful measuring is required.

**3.** Each side must also be routed on one end to form a groove for the end frame/slide to fit. This process will take more than one pass with the 1/16-in. straight-cut router bit. Set the fence for the first pass so that the 1/16-in. router bit's cut will be equal in distance to the depth of the rabbet on the ends of the end frame/slide. Then widen the cut slightly by moving the fence a hair away from the bit. Sneak up on a perfect fit. Use an end frame/slide to check that the tongue fits the sides. When your end grooves are perfectly formed, the end frame/slide will move easily in the tracks formed in the box sides, and it will fit flush with the ends of the box's inner sides (**PHOTO C**).

# Assemble the box

**NOW THAT WE'VE CUT THE SIDE AND END** pieces and cut all the necessary grooves in the inner sides, it is time to assemble them.

**1.** Begin assembling the box by gluing the inner box sides to the veneered outer box sides. The excess width of the outer sides should extend beyond the inner sides on the top side, which is the same side that the grooves for the lids were cut. Be careful that the bottom edge of the outer side is closely aligned with the bottom edge of the inner side, so that only a small amount will need to be trimmed from the outer side to make them flush (**PHOTO A**). I use the router table with a flush routing bit to even the edge of the veneered outer side with the inner sides (**PHOTO B**).

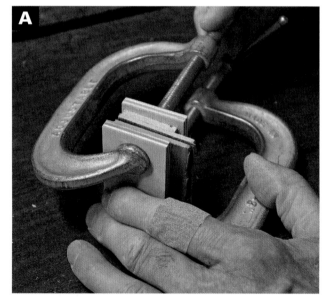

GLUE THE INNER SIDES of the box to the material that you veneered to form the outer sides. These veneered outer panels are much larger than the inner ones to accommodate the larger width of the bottom with some extra material to spare.

**2.** Trim the sides of the outer sides flush to the inner sides using the sled on the tablesaw and a stop block that is notched to allow clearance for the excess material (**PHOTO C**).

**3.** Use the sled on the tablesaw to cut the track housing and inner and outer ends to length (**PHOTO D**).

**B**

USE A FLUSH TRIMMING BIT in the router table to cut the outer side flush with the bottom edge of the inner side.

**C**

USE THE TABLESAW and sled to trim the ends of the outer sides flush with the ends of the inner sides. Note the small cutout in the stop block, which allows the ends of the veneered outer sides to slip under so the stop block only touches the ends of the inner stock.

USE THE TABLESAW AND SLED to cut the inner and outer ends and track housing to length.

**D**

**GLUE THE INNER END** to the box sides. I use a track housing (unglued) to support one end of the assembly and a block cut to the same length to stabilize the assembly as I bring all the parts into alignment.

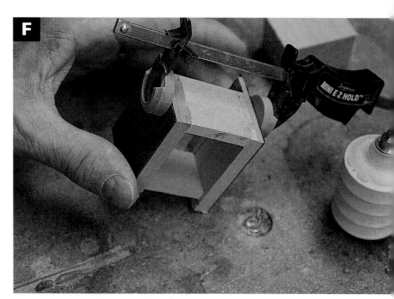

**APPLY CLAMPING PRESSURE** to hold the box in shape as the glue sets. The track housing is loose, but in place to secure the shape.

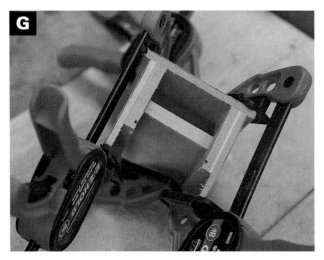

**ONCE THE INNER END IS GLUED** in place, the bottom can be glued on. Keep the track housing in place but unglued as the clamps hold the assembly in shape.

**4.** Apply glue to the ends of the inner end and align them with the ends of the glued-up box sides. Note that I put the track housing in place but don't glue it at this point, as it and the track it hides will be glued in place later in the assembly process. I use a spacer block of the same length to help steady the assembly until a clamp can be applied to hold the back to the sides **(PHOTO E )**. When the edges are carefully aligned, remove the spacer block and set the parts aside for an hour or so as the glue sets **(PHOTO F )**.

**5.** Glue the bottom of the box in place. I leave it slightly overhanging in all directions so that the edges can be trimmed flush after the glue sets. To make sure the box dimensions are not distorted in the gluing operation, keep the track housing in place as a spacer **(PHOTO G )**.

**6.** After the glue has set, use a piloted flush trimming bit in the router table to trim the bottom edges flush with the sides and end **(PHOTO H )**.

**7.** Use a belt sander or flat sheet of sandpaper on the workbench to flatten the end of the box in preparation for the addition of the veneered outer end **(PHOTO I )**.

**8.** Apply glue to the end of the box (this is the non-operative end) and then glue the veneered outer end to the inner end. The outer end should extend beyond all edges so that it can be trimmed flush after the lid is in place **(PHOTO J )**.

**USE THE ROUTER TABLE** and a flush-cut piloted router bit to trim the bottom of the box even with the sides and inner end.

**LIGHTLY SAND THE BACK** of the box to prepare for the veneered outer panel to be added to it, being careful not to distort the sides by excessive sanding. This can also be done using a flat sheet of sandpaper on the bench top.

**GLUE THE OUTER END** of the box in place. Apply glue to the inner end and to the ends of the veneered sides.

# Make the sliding lid

**THE SLIDING LID FOR THIS BOX CONSISTS OF** two parts. The inner part has a tongue that allows it to slide in the box sides. The outer part is veneered and cut to fit the width of the opening between the outer sides and cut to the length of the opening from the back of the box to the front of the sides.

**1.** Now that the first part of the assembly process is complete, the inner lid can be carefully shaped and fitted. Measure the width of the opening between the two outer layers of the box and add to it the depths of the grooves cut in the box sides. Rip $5/32$-in.-thick material to that width. In the photo below, the test piece just fits **(PHOTO A )**.

**2.** Cut the inner lid to length using the sled on the tablesaw. Because I always make multiple boxes and duplicate pieces in case of failure, I use a stop block to make certain that each is cut to the same length **(PHOTO B )**.

**3.** Next, form tongues on each side of the inner lid that will fit in the grooves cut in the sides of the box. I set the height of the tablesaw at about $1/16$ in. and set the fence so that there is a $1/16$-in. space between it and the blade. Note the plywood on top of the tablesaw: Just as in forming the grooves in the box sides, it is laid down on top of the saw to provide zero-clearance support for this

**MEASURE THE WIDTH** of the inner lid carefully. Here I'm checking the width of my stock to see how it fits in the total space formed by the grooves cut in the inner box sides.

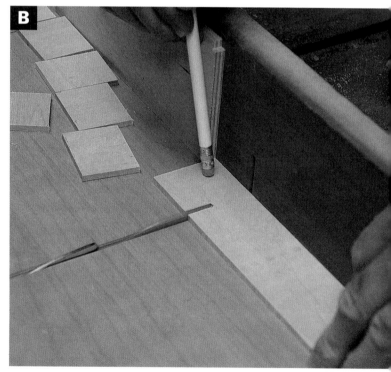

**USE THE TABLESAW SLED** to cut the inner lid to final length.

operation (**PHOTO C**). Use a notched push block to hold the lid assembly tight to the fence and to keep your fingers a safe distance from the blade.

**4.** When the inner lid is fitted and slides in and out without much friction, the veneered outer lid panel can be glued to it. Trim the veneered panel to fit in the space between the outer sides, outer end, and front of the box.

**5.** With the inner lid in place in the box, apply glue to the inner lid and clamp the veneered outer lid panel to it (**PHOTO D**). Use a clamp to secure them together. After the glue has begun to set, pull the still-clamped inner lid out of the box so it does not become glued permanently in place (**PHOTO E**).

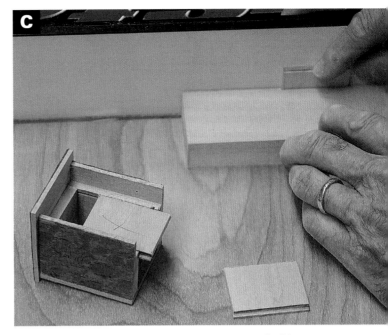

**USE THE TABLESAW** to form a tongue on each side of the inner lid, with the size of the tongue fitted to the grooves on the inner sides of the box. The box in the foreground shows the intended effect.

**CUT THE VENEERED OUTER LID** to fit the opening. Then spread glue on the inner lid and glue the outer lid to it.

**USE A CLAMP** to hold the outer veneered lid to the inner lid as the glue dries. But move the lid out of position as the glue sets to avoid having excess glue set the lid permanently in place.

# Assemble the hidden track

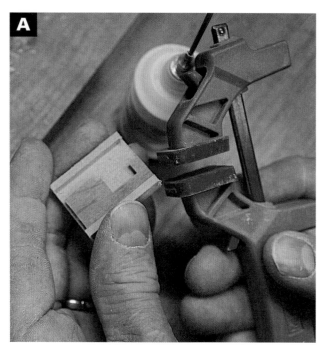

**GLUE THE TRACK** in the track housing. Keep the edges aligned on the right as shown.

**USE THE SLED** to cut the slide stop and the slide block to length. These are small parts, so I use a pencil to hold the parts tightly against the stop block.

**THE HIDDEN TRACK ON THE INSIDE OF THE** box consists of the track housing, the track, and the slide stop.

**1.** Glue the track to the inside of the track housing, being careful to align both parts on the right (**PHOTO A**).

**2.** Cut the tiny slide stop piece from a thin strip of wood. Because it is so small, you may simply cut it to length with a chisel. If using the tablesaw, use the sled and the point of a pencil to hold it in position during the cut (**PHOTO B**). Then glue the slide stop in place, with one end aligned with the upper right edge of the track housing.

**3.** Only slightly larger is the slide block, which you can cut to length on the tablesaw using the sled. Make a shallow relief cut along one edge at each side, as shown in the drawing on p, 143, so that any excess glue used in installing it will not permanently lock the box in a closed position.

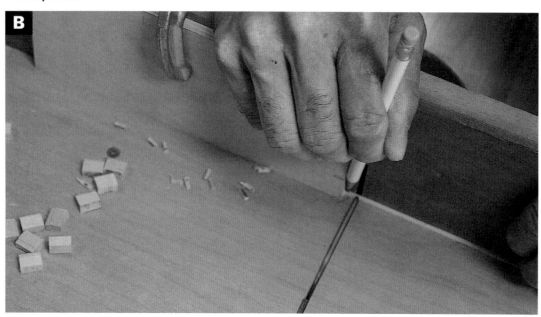

**4.** Use the tablesaw to cut the upper and lower operable ends and the center slide. With the table-saw blade tilted to 22½ degrees, cut the parts to the dimensions given in the materials list. If you are careful in making these cuts, the upper and lower operable end pieces and the center slide can be cut from the same piece of veneered stock. The center piece will slide between the two outside parts. Use a push block to safely cut these small parts **(PHOTO C )**.

**USE THE TABLESAW** with the angle set at 22½ degrees to rip the operable end parts and center slide from a single piece of veneered stock. A zero-clearance surface laid over the top of the saw helps in the cutting of such small stock. Use a push block to move stock safely through the cut.

# Finish the assembly

**NOW THAT WE'VE ASSEMBLED THE BOX AND** cut the rest of the puzzle box mechanism pieces, we can finish putting together the puzzle mechanism.

**1.** Glue the end frame/slide to the upper and lower operable end parts, with the center slide in place to control the spacing between **(PHOTO A)**. As clamping pressure is applied, be careful that the center slide is slightly offset from its confining parts. Slide it back and forth slightly to be sure it is not being fixed in place by excess glue **(PHOTO B)**.

**2.** Glue the slide block to the center slide. Be careful while doing this that both ends of the center slide are aligned with its mates and that the sliding block is positioned as shown in the photo below right **(PHOTO C)**. Apply glue to the thinner side of the sliding block and clamp it in place until the glue dries, as shown on the facing page **(PHOTO D)**.

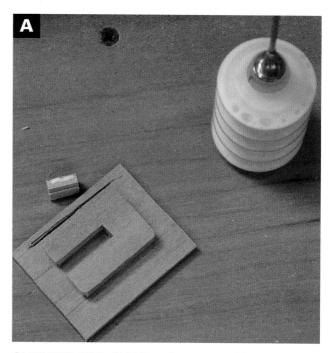

**GLUE THE END SLIDE** to the upper and lower operable ends of the box, leaving the center slide unglued so it can slide between. Note the slide block ready to be glued in place.

**CLAMP THE END FRAME/SLIDE** to the upper and lower operable ends as the glue sets.

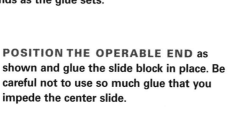

**POSITION THE OPERABLE END** as shown and glue the slide block in place. Be careful not to use so much glue that you impede the center slide.

**3.** Slide the operable end into place. Then apply glue to the ends of the track housing and glue it in place. This must be done with the operable end in the fully closed position, as shown below **(PHOTO E)**. You will need to adjust the operable end slightly to position the slide block to fit in the track.

**4.** After the glue has set, move the operable end into its lowest position so the top can slide into place. If the operable end does not move low enough for the lid to slide in place, as is the case in the photo on p. 166 **(PHOTO F)**, raise the operable end high enough to trim material from the top edge. This can be done with a handplane, sanding block, or saw, but in order to move the operable end up you will need to follow the steps required to open the finished box (see the sidebar on p. 167).

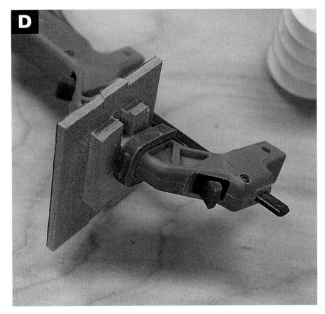

**WHILE THE GLUE IS SETTING,** clamp the slide block in place.

**SPREAD GLUE ON THE ENDS** of the track housing after all the internal parts are in place. The operable end should be in its closed position with the center slide aligned with the outside edges. You will have to move the operable end up and down just a bit as you nest the track housing in place with one side flat to the bottom of the box.

**F**

**IF THE LID DOESN'T FIT** trim the operable end just enough for the lid to pass into the grooves cut in the inner sides. This can be done with a plane, sanding block, or saw.

**5.** With the lid in place and the box in a closed position, trim the edges at the top of the box so they rise only slightly higher than the height of the lid, then sand the surfaces flush. This can be done on a belt sander or with a sanding block.

**6.** Use a ⅛-in. radius roundover bit in the router table to round the edges, using a guide piece on the outside to hold the slide in place as you do so. This will prevent it from pushing in or out and being cut too deep **(PHOTO G )**.

**7.** When the box is complete, sand using 180-grit, 240-grit, and 320-grit. Veneered boxes present a special challenge in that a great deal of attention is required to keep from sanding through the veneer. You will likely find that sanding on a flat sheet of sandpaper rather than with a power sander will help you to avoid sanding through. Change hand position frequently to prevent sanding too much from one angle. Apply Danish oil to your finished box.

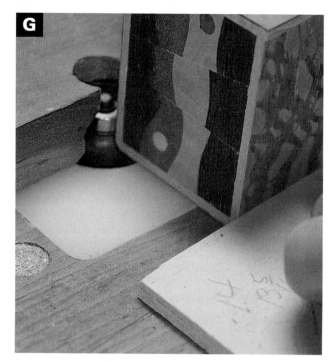

**G**

**USE THE ROUTER TABLE** and ⅛-in.-radius roundover bit to smooth the edges of the box before sanding.

# HOW TO OPEN THE BOX

Here is the full sequence of steps to open the box. These are hidden from view when the box is fully assembled.

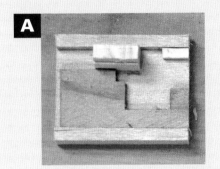

In **A** the slide block is in the closed position and if observed from outside the box, the center slide would be aligned with the edges of the sides.

Sliding the center slide moves the slide block against the tiny slide stop at right **B**.

Sliding the slide block down and to the right allows the end of the box to slide down in **C**.

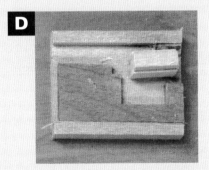

Once down, the slide block can slide further to the right **D**.

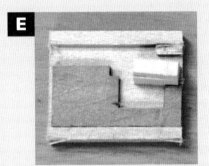

In **E** the end of the box has been moved down a second time.

The end moving down allows the slide block to slide back to the left **F**.

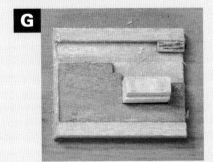

Sliding the slide block to the left allows the end of the box to slide down a third time **G**, providing just enough clearance for the slid to slide open.

# Resources

**RARE EARTH MAGNETS**
**K&J Magnetics, Inc.**
A full selection of rare earth magnets
www.kjmagnetics.com

**HARDWARE FOR BOXMAKING**
**Lee Valley Tools**
www.LeeValley.com

**Rockler Woodworking and**
**Hardware**
Stores and catalog
www.Rockler.com

**Woodcraft Supply**
Stores and catalog
www.Woodcraft.com

Your local hardware store or
building supply

**GENERAL WOODWORKING**
**INFORMATION**
*Fine Woodworking*
www.Finewoodworking.com

**DOUG STOWE'S BOOKS IN PRINT**
Available from www.tauntonstore.com
*Taunton's Complete Illustrated Guide to*
   *Box Making*
*Basic Box Making*
*Rustic Furniture Basics*
*Building Small Cabinets*
*Beautiful Boxes*

**DOUG STOWE'S DVDS**
Available from www.tauntonstore.com
*Basic Box Making*
*Rustic Furniture Basics*
*Building Small Cabinets*

**DOUG STOWE'S BLOGS**
Boxmaking101.blogspot.com
WisdomofHands.blogspot.com

**DOUG STOWE'S WEBSITES**
Boxmaking101.com
DougStowe.com

**WHERE TO GET WOOD**
Where to get wood is the question that
my students always ask. I consider the
finding and acquisition of wood for
building boxes to be one of the great
adventures of woodworking. It's an
adventure that's led me down narrow
country lanes in search of sawmills that
offer interesting, beautiful local woods.
Would it be right for me to deprive
my readers of the adventure that I've
enjoyed so much?

You can find wonderful woods for sale
on eBay and other websites that can
be delivered to your door. But most
of the wood I use for making boxes
comes from offcuts and leftovers from
larger works. I have to admit to being a
hoarder of beautiful woods, and because
of that, no woods were purchased in the
making of this book, or I would have
been able to tell you, my dear readers,
where to buy. Instead, I will direct you
to the best information available for
your own small local community.

Look for woodworking clubs in
your city or town. I have taught in
woodworking clubs all across the U.S.
and I've found them to be the Mount
Everest of woodworking information.
You will be astounded by the willingness
of other woodworkers to share sources
and materials. I have found amateur
woodworkers to be the most generous
of our human kind. Whether in a club
or not, look for other woodworkers in
your community, share what you are
learning and your enthusiasm for it, and
you will find support, friends, and even
free lumber on occasion.

# Metric Equivalents

| Inches | Centimeters | Millimeters | | Inches | Centimeters | Millimeters |
|--------|-------------|-------------|---|--------|-------------|-------------|
| ⅛ | 0.3 | 3 | | 13 | 33.0 | 330 |
| ¼ | 0.6 | 6 | | 14 | 35.6 | 356 |
| ⅜ | 1.0 | 10 | | 15 | 38.1 | 381 |
| ½ | 1.3 | 13 | | 16 | 40.6 | 406 |
| ⅝ | 1.6 | 16 | | 17 | 43.2 | 432 |
| ¾ | 1.9 | 19 | | 18 | 45.7 | 457 |
| ⅞ | 2.2 | 22 | | 19 | 48.3 | 483 |
| 1 | 2.5 | 25 | | 20 | 50.8 | 508 |
| 1¼ | 3.2 | 32 | | 21 | 53.3 | 533 |
| 1½ | 3.8 | 38 | | 22 | 55.9 | 559 |
| 1¾ | 4.4 | 44 | | 23 | 58.4 | 584 |
| 2 | 5.1 | 51 | | 24 | 61.0 | 610 |
| 2½ | 6.4 | 64 | | 25 | 63.5 | 635 |
| 3 | 7.6 | 76 | | 26 | 66.0 | 660 |
| 3½ | 8.9 | 89 | | 27 | 68.6 | 686 |
| 4 | 10.2 | 102 | | 28 | 71.1 | 711 |
| 4½ | 11.4 | 114 | | 29 | 73.7 | 737 |
| 5 | 12.7 | 127 | | 30 | 76.2 | 762 |
| 6 | 15.2 | 152 | | 31 | 78.7 | 787 |
| 7 | 17.8 | 178 | | 32 | 81.3 | 813 |
| 8 | 20.3 | 203 | | 33 | 83.8 | 838 |
| 9 | 22.9 | 229 | | 34 | 86.4 | 864 |
| 10 | 25.4 | 254 | | 35 | 88.9 | 889 |
| 11 | 27.9 | 279 | | 36 | 91.4 | 914 |
| 12 | 30.5 | 305 | | | | |